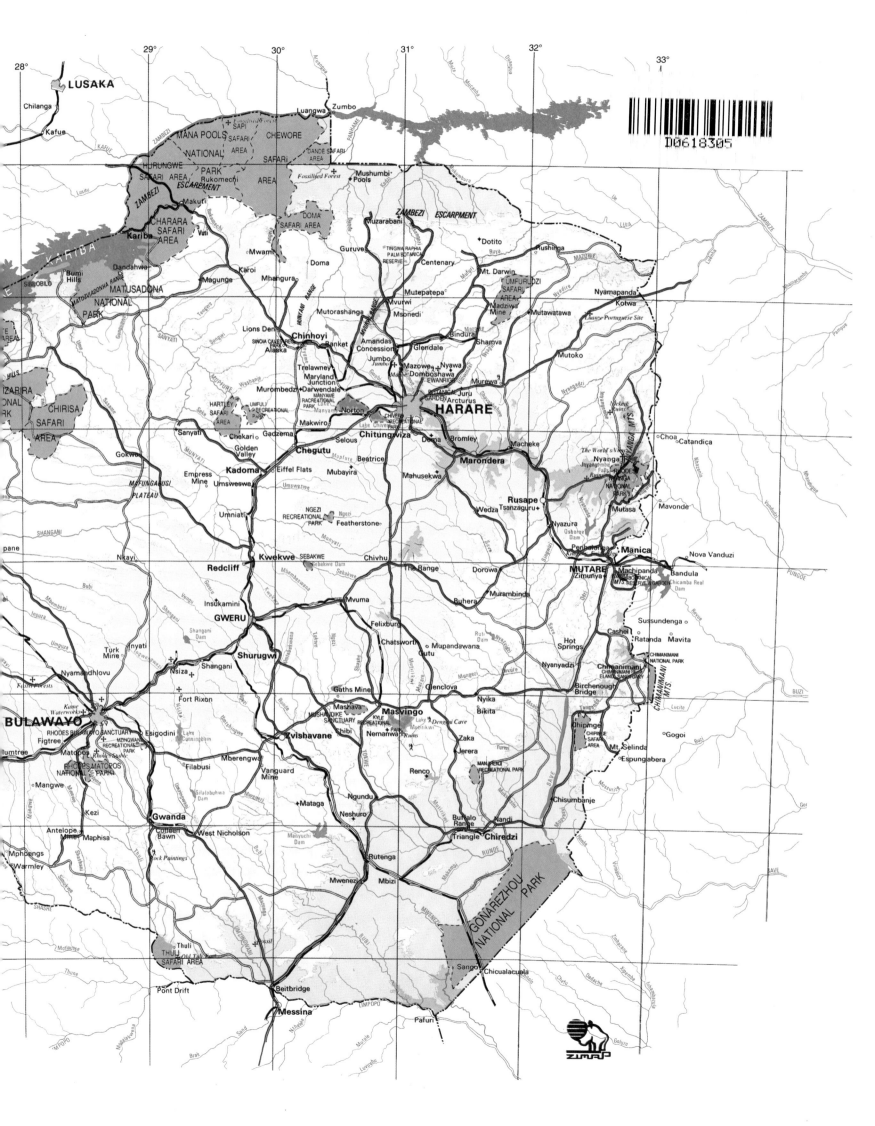

ZIMBABWE
AFRICA'S PARADISE

PHOTOGRAPHY BY IAN MURPHY

WRITTEN BY RICHARD VAUGHAN

ISBN No. 0 9515209 3 8

Publisher
CBC Publishing
36 Finborough Road
London SW10 9EG

Distribution by:
Roundhouse
PO Box 140
Oxford OX2 7SF
Telephone: 44 (0) 865 512682
Fax: 44 (0) 865 59594

Design
Pilcher Graphics Limited
PO Box 30806
Lusaka, Zambia
and
Barney Wan
London

Printed in Singapore

Other Titles available:
ZAMBIA
by Richard Vaughan and Ian Murphy

THE SPIRIT OF THE ZAMBEZI
by Jeff and Veronica Stutchbury

ACKNOWLEDGMENTS

Every photograph in this book is the result of collaboration and help from the people of Zimbabwe. While it would be impossible to mention everyone by name, we would particularly like to highlight the following for their crucial assistance.

Enos Chiura of the Delta Corporation immediately recognised the possibilities of our proposal and with his team, Patrick Rooney, Pip Maxwell, Ron Stringfellow and Alastair Wright spared no effort in making this publication possible.

By supplying transport, and giving us access to many facets of Zimbabwe's economic life, Lonrho supported this venture more than generously. We would particularly like to thank Chris Parvin and Errol Tillett, in Harare, Paul Spicer and Jim Hughes in London for their support.

The warmth and friendliness of Zimbabweans in all walks of life was quite extraordinary. Andrew Mutandwa at the High Commission in London watched over the project as it developed and gave considered and much appreciated advice. My shamwari Stewart Mushayakarara made the months of travelling most enjoyable. Ralph, Gerry and all the Stuchbury family helped in every way they could. David and Marcey Key, and Peter and Jutta Jackson, did the same. Sandros, John Edlin and Angus Shaw helped to keep the project well oiled. William Ruck-Keene of Tongabezi and his microlight helped with the aerial picture of Victoria Falls.

Jerusha Arothe-Vaughan was instrumental in getting the project off the ground, and conducted much invaluable research. Tracey Derrick, Louise Erasmus and Leslie Malkin, all helped with the London administration of the project. Danny Pope edited the photographs and helped to achieved the accuracy of the colour. Mick Pilcher and Barney Wan worked long hours to meet the deadlines of this publication.

The Ministry of Information, the Commercial Farmers Union, the CZI, the Ministry of Justice all gave invaluable comments on the text, as did the National Archives, whose book, *Zimbabwe Epic* proved an invaluable source of historical information.

FOREWORD

Zimbabwe's history and natural beauty have conspired to give the global community a very limited view of what our country has to offer. To many it is still remembered as a nation of violence and interminable political wrangling, while others who come here may find themselves seeing little more than the natural wonders on display in the National Parks. In both cases, outsiders may have learnt little in recent years about the lives of Zimbabweans themselves.

The express purpose of this book is to portray the *other* Zimbabwe, a country of people at work and at play, with dreams and aspirations which so rarely get an airing in the outside world. Space has of course been made for the Victoria Falls, the Hwange Game Reserve and the ruins of Great Zimbabwe, but more significant are the factories, farms, forests, schools and hospitals which our people created, and which keep them busy from dawn till dusk. It has taken Ian Murphy and Richard Vaughan nearly two years to record such a heritage, and when it is condensed between the covers of a single volume the richness and potential of our country are instantly apparent.

At the same time this is not a propaganda piece. The problems we face, be they economic, social or environmental, are all squarely addressed, but they are put in a positive context which reveals the resources available to deal with them. After a thorough perusal I hope the reader will come away with a deeper understanding of what all Zimbabweans have struggled to achieve, and of what this nation can give, not just to its own people, but to the world at large.

R.G. MUGABE
PRESIDENT OF THE REPUBLIC OF ZIMBABWE

ZIMBABWE

AFRICA'S PARADISE

CONTENTS

INTRODUCTION

Zimbabwe shines like a jewel among the nations of Africa. For although this country has been through the familiar traumas of colonisation, war and factional in-fighting, it has emerged intact, almost uniquely amongst post-colonial African countries as a viable economy with a genuine parliamentary process, an independent judiciary, freedom of speech and stable race relations.

This book is a celebration of Zimbabwe, a portrait of a nation with a strong industrial infrastructure, agricultural economy, cultural identity and sense of direction. While it is essentially a picture book, 'Zimbabwe' is designed to give unacquainted visitors enough information on the country to get their bearings. The term visitors is used advisedly, for tourists represent a fraction of those who come to the country each year. While the book should undoubtedly be useful to them, it is also aimed at diplomats, industrialists and others who may want to forge professional links with the country. In the following pages we have tried to include a little of everything, so that a thorough browse can give the reader a well-rounded perspective or feel of the country.

But this book is not simply aimed at visitors. Zimbabweans themselves may find within its pages unfamiliar images - pictures which offer fresh insights into life in their homeland. Too often in the past, coffee-table books on Africa depict it as a continent to be revelled in by affluent foreigners, and while it may be laudable to portray a breathtaking world of mountains, rivers, game and other natural wonders this is a very one-dimensional view. We have thus made every effort to show the other Zimbabwe - a country of farms, forests and factories which form the backbone of the nation's economy. Zimbabwe is blessed with a fine climate, good soils and over forty different minerals. Consequently its infrastructure has some features which are outstanding in Africa.

The industrial base is exceptionally diverse, comprising activities as varied as food processing and packaging, the manufacture of metal goods, chemical and petroleum products as well as drink, tobacco and textiles. Mining also plays a vital role in the economy; gold, asbestos, nickel, copper, coal and chrome are all extracted in abundance. The agricultural sector is just as diverse as the country's industry, with tobacco, tea, maize, cotton, wheat, sugar and coffee as the major crops. Beef and dairy farming are also important. To service such a variety of activities there is a wide range of banking institutions, insurance companies and pension funds as well as an active capital market with the Zimbabwe Stock Exchange at its hub.

For transport and communications, Zimbabwe must be the envy of many African states. Despite the damage done during the war there has been a vigorous building programme since 1980. Most road construction has been concentrated on providing access to the communal farming areas, which had previously been quite isolated. The road network now has one of the highest densities in sub-Saharan Africa and continues to grow each year. The railway system runs through the nation's borders at all points of the compass and connects all major cities, while the giant marshalling yards at Bulawayo and Gweru are among the largest in Africa.

It would scarcely do the country justice to ignore such remarkable achievements as these, attained against tremendous odds. Our aim has been to portray every sphere of life in the country, so we have devoted much more space to the nation's economic life than is normally done by books of this nature. Wildlife and scenery have their place too, but we have focused mainly on human activity. Zimbabwe is nothing without its people, and the people spend most of their waking hours at work.

This introduction deals with the country's recorded social history. Like the history of most African states it is a story of an indigenous people being overrun by the greater economic strength of outsiders before finally acquiring self-determination through political struggle. It is also the story of a fusion of cultures, of an indigenous civilisation absorbing the characteristics of the very influences which it sought to dispel. Zimbabwe's modern history, while owing a great deal to the Shona and Ndebele cultures, is also peppered with ideologies from Europe and the Arab world - market capitalism, Christianity, Islam, Marxism and parliamentary democracy, to name but a few.

THE FIRST CONTACT

Like much of the rest of Africa, Zimbabwe betrays evidence of a vigorous social life which goes back thousands of years. But as with most pre-colonial civilisations, those which flourished in this pocket of the continent did so without the help of the written word. Consequently, whilst it is possible to deduce much about the way of life of ancient tribes, virtually nothing can be gleaned about specific events which took place before the arrival of outsiders.

The first foreigners to break in on the ancient land which lay between the Limpopo and the Zambezi were not Europeans, but Arabs. Between the tenth and sixteenth centuries, East Coast Moslems traded extensively with the indigenous people. However, no attempt was made to colonise or subjugate them.

When the Portuguese arrived in the early sixteenth century the situation began to alter decisively, for territory became another means of strategic exchange. By now the land that was to become Zimbabwe was dominated by the Mutapa dynasty. They ran a state system which owed much to the earlier culture of Great Zimbabwe itself, described in detail in the first chapter of this book. Despite internal conflicts, the Mutapa state was both wealthy and powerful, relying on cattle, agriculture and trade for its well-being. It was in the 1570s that the Portuguese tried to attack and control it. The attempt failed, forcing the Portuguese to resort to less direct means of control. Skillful political manoeuvring rewarded them in 1629 with a treaty which effectively made them rulers of the state, working through officials acceptable to them. Conversion to Christianity through Dominican priests was one of the criteria of acceptability. In the face of threats from their compatriots it was only possible for the local rulers to survive with the military backing of the Portuguese.

Things began to change in the 1680s and 90s with the emergence of a new and powerful Shona state to the south west the Rozvi people under the Changamire dynasty, who had been former subjects of the Mutapa. In the face of threats that the Portuguese might intensify and extend their control, the Mutapa and Changamire states eventually united. In 1693, they succeeded in driving the Portuguese out, and from then onwards the Portuguese role in the area was reduced to a commercial one, like that of their Arab predecessors.

The next wave of foreign territorial interest came a hundred and fifty years later, and it was not the Shona people, but the Ndebele, who were to bear the brunt of it. Living to the south west of the Shona, the Ndebele were an altogether different people. Husbandry and crop raising satisfied only part of their needs; raiding other peoples for their cattle, and food supplied the rest. Their social cement was not the occupation of a common territory so much as membership of a highly disciplined military system, with the king as supreme commander, holding autocratic power of life and death over his subjects. They lived within an 80 kilometre radius of a royal kraal near modern Bulawayo, from which base raiding parties were dispatched among the Shona. When, in the 1890s, Europeans came into their territory in large numbers, the Ndebele were still raiding Shona land to the west of present day Harare and around Great Zimbabwe.

The Europeans themselves were a new factor in the equation, and they were not a welcome one to the Ndebele. Their king, Mzilikazi, could see clearly that the presence of white men in his territory would pose a powerful foreign threat. But he was prepared to grant one modest concession. In 1859, he allowed the son of an old friend, Robert Moffat, to establish a mission station on his land. It was a second concession, nine years later, which was to prove much more decisive. Just before he died Mzilikazi allowed a few white hunters to shoot elephant in his domain. One of them was a certain Henry Hartley, who in the course of his sport chanced upon some ancient gold workings. The news spread like wildfire right down to the Cape, where Europeans had been arriving in droves to prospect for gold. By now, Mzilikazi was dead. His son, Lobengula found himself besieged by white concession seekers. A few traders were admitted and permission was given for small groups of Boers (descendants of earlier Dutch settlers in the Cape) to make expeditions into his territory. With a couple of notable exceptions, they were to be disappointed, and they either drifted home or lingered in the growing community of prospectors and adventurers petitioning for Lobengula's favour.

THE ARRIVAL OF MR RHODES

Despite the paucity of large gold deposits, other natural resources were discovered, among them an abundance of rich farmland under a perfect climate. For Lobengula, the writing was on the wall. Europe's 'Scramble for Africa' was under way. Portuguese, British, Spanish, Germans, Dutch and Belgians as well as Transvaal Republicans were all looking lustfully at the land which lay to the north of the Limpopo.

The most predatory of them all was an Englishman by the name of Cecil John Rhodes. By any standards he was a remarkable figure. The son of a country vicar, he was born in the tiny provincial village of Saffron Walden in Essex. At the age of seventeen, Rhodes travelled to Africa to improve his health, and made a huge fortune in diamonds within two years. By the time he reached his early thirties he had become a political force to be reckoned with, both in Africa and Britain. His acquisitive spirit extended well beyond the desire for money: his ultimate goal was a railway spanning the entire continent of Africa, from the Cape in the south to Cairo in the north, all of it built through territory coloured pink on the map to denote British possession.

Lobengula had inherited his father's shrewd and pragmatic attitude to foreigners, but the tide of world history was running against him. The land which he believed was his by right of conquest Rhodes now plotted to take from him through stealth or force, whichever was to prove the more effective. When, in 1887, Rhodes heard that Lobengula was allowing a large number of Transvaal farmers to hunt in his territory he sensed an impending settlement with the Boers. The time had come to act.

During this time, treaties which Europeans drew with African sovereigns were not designed to promote accord between the two parties. Instead, they were implemented to furnish the Europeans with a basis in international law for pre-empting other interested parties. In 1888, it was John Moffat, the missionary, who obtained for Rhodes a treaty in which Lobengula vowed not to enter into any agreement with another power without British approval. The effect of such a treaty was ultimately to bring Matabeleland into the British sphere of influence, and to keep other Europeans out.

Later that year Rhodes was able to go further. His business partner, Charles Rudd, apparently managed to persuade Lobengula to grant "complete and exclusive" right to all minerals in his Kingdom, principalities and domains, together with full power to do all things that they may deem necessary to win and procure same. Lobengula, however, had agreed to the Concession on verbal undertakings by Rudd that it would protect his people from further European pressure, and that only ten Europeans would enter his territory to work the mines. Not only that, but these men were to operate under Ndebele law and would be liable for military service with the Ndebele should Lobengula be attacked. In fact, none of these undertakings was written into the Concession, and the pledges were deliberately ignored by Rhodes and his compatriots, who proceeded to form the British South Africa Company in London with the express purpose of making British subjects richer at the expense of local Africans. The year after he had put his mark on the agreement, Lobengula sent two envoys to London to revoke it, having realised the extent to which he had been duped. His efforts were fruitless. On 29 October 1889, the British South Africa Company received a charter from the British Crown authorising it to go about its business.

In desperation, Lobengula found reasons for postponing the entry of outsiders into his territory. But although the Concession included no right to land, it did confer the right of access to its minerals, and therefore occupation. A deliberate fiction was concocted, that all Mashonaland *in addition* to the land of the Ndebele came under Lobengula's domain and thus fell within the Concession. On this basis, the occupation of Mashonaland was planned.

Rhodes shrewdly decided that this should by done by a route well to the east of Matabeleland proper. Thus, if Lobengula left them alone, he would be seen to be sanctioning the move. But if he attacked, Rhodes would have a pretext for destroying him. Lobengula knew that he stood no chance if he tried to fight, so he let the column pass.

On September 13, 1890, two hundred hand-picked pioneers and twice their number in Company Policemen completed their 700 kilometre march from the south and raised the British flag on an empty plain right in the middle of Mashonaland. It was land which had once been under the influence of a prominent Shona chief called Harare. But the fort which the British built was named after their Prime Minister, Lord Salisbury.

In vain, Lobengula tried to play rival European interests off against one another by granting the Lippert Concession, an agreement which gave the Germans land rights throughout his domain. Rhodes forestalled him. He simply bought the concession from Lippert, thus obtaining a form of title to the land in addition to the one he already had to its mineral wealth.

So monstrously had Rhodes behaved that a violent showdown was inevitable. By now, Lobengula was under strong pressure from his young warriors to drive the Europeans out of his country. At the same time members of the Company, who felt threatened by the Ndebele, were spoiling for a fight. A pretext presented itself in October 1893 when a minor disagreement over cattle prompted an inter-tribal skirmish instigated by the Ndebele. The Company claimed that as the Shona were living under its protection, it was obliged to take action against the Ndebele king. Armed columns of irregulars, with promises of thirty gold claims and 2,420 hectares of farmland for every man at the end of the campaign, closed in on Lobengula from three separate directions. Lobengula's weapons were no match for the Company's Maxim machine guns. By the end of battle, on November 4th 1890, the Europeans were standing among the smouldering ruins of Lobengula's royal kraal at Bulawayo.

Lobengula, who had put his own city to the torch, fled northwards. But a force was dispatched in hot pursuit. In his wake, the hapless king sent messages of peace and a bag of gold sovereigns as a token of good will, but the gold was appropriated by some troopers and the messages were not relayed to the British commanding officer. Then, on the Shangani River, the British received reports that Lobengula was nearby on the opposite bank and, although it was late in the day, a reconnaissance patrol under Major Allan Wilson was sent across. Cut off from the main force during the night by the rising waters of the Shangani, Wilson and his thirty four men found themselves next morning grouped around an ant hill in a mopane forest, surrounded by 3,000 Ndebele warriors. Even the most detached observer might argue that they deserved no mercy. In any event, they didn't get it.

Several weeks after the pursuit at the Shangani was abandoned, news reached Bulawayo that Lobengula had died somewhere in the north. His young sons were spirited off to the Cape under the pretext of getting an education, so that there could be no claimants to the Ndebele throne. The extension of Company rule to Matabeleland brought a boom in prospecting, mining, farming and speculation. Within two years, Bulawayo, with three thousand Europeans, had become the largest settlement in the country. On the crest of a commercial wave in 1895, the land of the Monomatapas and the Rozvi Mambos was officially renamed Rhodesia.

When violent resistance to the occupation began a year later, all sorts of explanations were offered, drought, rinderpest and locusts among them, but the most plausible of all is the self-deception of the settlers themselves. They were apparently quite convinced that the Ndebele, with a long-standing reputation for military prowess, had meekly submitted to a labouring role. Furthermore, in a pattern which was repeated the length and breadth of Africa, they believed that the Shona were grateful to them for their deliverance from generations of harassment at the hands of the Ndebele. So complete was the faith which the conquerors had in the inherent superiority of their own values, that they had no hesitation in demanding taxes from the Shona for the express purpose of upholding the new order.

Nor, apparently, were any moral qualms expressed about the immediate suspension of a long-standing and amicable trade in gold which the Shona had enjoyed with the Portuguese.

Nor did it occur to the settlers that there might be bitter resentment at the seizure of local land and its redistribution to their own farmers.

It is easy to make moral judgments about a man like Cecil Rhodes from the perspective of the late twentieth century. By today's standards – whatever else he may have been – Rhodes was a bully, a liar and a thief. In his own lifetime, he was simply operating within the cultural norms of nineteenth century Europe.

It was a world in which Darwin's theories had been popularised in such a way that the white man was placed just below God at the top of the Great Chain of Being, with other peoples taking their place at various points below him. It was a world in which the most recent strides in engineering and technology had put Britain ahead of all other nations on earth. It was also a world in which it seemed perfectly natural for a young man, raised with the best education available, to feel a sense of mission in 'civilising' peoples on another continent, while at the same time filling the coffers of his Queen's treasury.

When Rhodes died in 1902, even The Times of London felt unable to give him an unequivocally fulsome obituary, finding his lust for power overbearing. But the paper was still able to declare that "...his countrymen will gratefully and proudly add his name to the distinguished roll of those who have made the British Empire what it is."

When the descendants of Africa's indigenous people come to write their own history, they are likely to judge him less kindly.

As it happened, white supremacy was to last only a few generations. Within ninety years – a mere sliver in the long history of Zimbabwe – the political kingdom would be back in black hands. As for the economic and cultural kingdoms, that is another story.

RHODESIA - THE EARLY YEARS

No sooner was the settler community truly established in Rhodesia than it was in serious danger of being wiped out. In March 1896, the Ndebele took up arms, followed in June the same year by their counterparts in Mashonaland. Isolation was the key to the effectiveness of the insurrection. Cut off from the rest of the world, Bulawayo and other towns had to 'go into laager', a state of siege. Reinforcements from South Africa and England soon arrived with cannon and machine guns, all of which were unavailable to the African insurgents. The rebels developed a system of hiding in caves, but dynamite was used to force them out. By the start of July, the outcome of the war was inevitable, and over the next two years the most important leaders were executed.

The rebellion has gone down in history as the First Chimurenga, the expression deriving from a Shona word which, roughly translated, means 'war of liberation'. Although the settlers were able to put it down decisively, it had been successful enough to force a number of concessions, including the removal of almost all Imperial troops from Matabeleland.

By the beginning of the twentieth century, the main pattern of development for the country had been laid down. The railway which had been part of Rhodes' dream ran from Cape Town to Bulawayo, then split in two directions: northwards to the Zambezi and eastwards to the Portuguese coast. The sites of all the principal towns had been established, and with few exceptions they followed the line of rail. Life within those townships was, in the words of an early woman settler, "civilised and suburban".

The sense of urgency and excitement which had pervaded the first waves of settlement gradually subsided, and the goal was no longer fame and fortune so much as survival itself. Life for white artisans, particularly those who worked on the railways or down the mines, could be tough. Sir Roy Welensky, who later scaled giddy heights as a politician, recalled a particularly gruelling youth. He went to school without shoes and swam, in his own words, "bare-arsed in the Makabusi". He never slept between sheets until he got married, nor owned a jacket until he was twenty. With his wife he shared two rooms with no kitchen, with a bathroom and toilet at the bottom of a field. He worked up to eighteen hours a day on the railway, and his first child died at nine months from enteritis, just one of the health hazards arising from the open drains.

Alongside miners, labourers and farmers, missionaries came into the newly established territory. From the outset, they were far more than advocates of their own Christian zeal. They practiced medicine, introducing new standards in hygiene and diet. They also taught industrial and domestic crafts, including carpentry, brick making, needlework and cookery. They started schools and worked out an orthography for African languages (which had previously only been spoken). Thus, the Bible and other books became available to a people who had little other chance of exposure to the outside world. A new generation of Africans began to learn British history and manners, nursery rhymes and games, of the sea and ships - indeed the whole background to an alien culture.

In remote areas, this was often achieved against tremendous odds. Disease and wild animals could exact a dreadful toll, but so absolute was the faith of these pioneers that the results of their efforts could be spectacular. One Native Commissioner who kept a diary while serving in the isolated Sebungwe area before the First World War recorded the following observations after visiting a local mission station: "It was astonishing what they had managed to do in view on the fact that every sheet of iron, and practically every other building material impossible to make locally, had been transported by carriers a distance of ninety miles from the nearest point on the railway. All buildings were of burnt brick under iron roofs with plenty of doors and windows, making them light and airy. Every desk and form had been made by Reverend Buckley and his pupils, while the floors were of cement, making for coolness and cleanliness.... The scholars I saw were spotlessly clean and most respectful in their demeanour."

Missionaries were swiftly followed by traders eager to bring in supplies. Sweets and new foods, knives and hatchets, oil lamps, mugs and metal pots, clocks, bicycles and matches – all became status symbols in the new order. As local desire for these novelties became keener so did the involvement with Europeans become ever more close, for they were the only source of the money needed to buy such goods. Young men whose fathers had been cattle herders or iron smelters became wage earners, either in domestic service or in the new industries which were now emerging.

Life under the British South Africa Company was hard for most local people. The Pass Laws and the Native Registration Laws were among the most repressive imposed by any colonial regime in Africa. In particular, they outlawed freedom of movement, making it very much easier for any insurrection to be kept at bay; a man could not move from his work-place without the written permission of his employer, nor could he travel without a pass issued by his local Pass Officer. A Registration Certificate also had to be carried if an African was to stay out of trouble.

The result of such restrictions was the availability of a cheap and largely immobile labour force which was put to use on the farms and down the mines of the colony. A new experience in poverty emerged, reminiscent in many ways of the Industrial Revolution in Europe. Entertainment in the workers' compounds was eventually provided with the advent of beer halls, but these were violent and vice-ridden places where prostitution and gambling were the common currency of social exchange. Apart from working conditions, the other great bone of contention was land. When it became clear to the colonial settlers that the prospect of easy gold was not going to live up to its promise, there was a surge of interest in farms for crops and cattle ranching. With military power now firmly in their hands, the acquisition of large tracts of the best farmland met with little resistance. Africans found themselves pushed out into less fertile areas where 'reserves' were established for them. Traditional shifting cultivation methods and unlimited pastures did not work so well under these conditions, and intensive efforts to work the soils made them even poorer. Locals also had to pay rents and taxes for the property which remained in their hands. Many were forced to sell their labour to the new employers in order to pay their way.

It was in this fertile soil that the first seeds of political activity were sewn. Miners, industrial workers, teachers, nurses and clerks coalesced to form a motley collection of unions. But while some had expressly political aims, others tended to be conservative and non-controversial.

While Africans struggled to find a voice, Rhodesia as a whole continued to prosper, all the more so with the arrival of the Second World War. Although Rhodesian territory was never threatened, the country was still involved out of loyalty to Britain. It had become a self-governing colony in 1923, but still retained close ties to the Crown. Many Rhodesians served in fighting units, but their chief contribution was to be in the supply of raw materials for the war effort. Such a policy laid the foundation for a post-war economic boom which, together with a huge increase in immigration from Europe and South Africa, changed a frugal society into an extravagant one. Salisbury in particular burst out of its municipal boundaries as spacious new suburbs sprang up. The open African skyline became closed off by hedges, trees and flowering shrubs, and the squat brick bungalows of the early years slowly gave way to concrete and glass.

THE FEDERATION

By the late 1940s there was a growing feeling in the colonial government that African nations were being left behind in the rush for economic expansion that was pervading the rest of the western world. Consequently some argued that Northern Rhodesia with its copper, and Southern Rhodesia with its coal, should forge some kind of union to take full advantage of their complementary economies. The two territories already possessed a common currency and a single railway system. This idea, which included the smaller territory of Nyasaland (now Malawi), offered a framework in which the white minority was able to retain the effective instruments of government for the foreseeable future. The Southern Rhodesian government was to have the lion's share of control, but the white communities in the other two states felt in a position to agree because they perceived clear economic and political advantages.

African protest at the proposal was vigorous, and political activists from all three territories lobbied strongly against the Federation, sending delegates to the first Federal Conference in London in 1952. But in spite of this opposition, the Federation of Rhodesia and Nyasaland was established on 4 September, 1953. Initially, the white populations on both sides of the Zambezi saw benefits. But as time went by it became clear that Southern Rhodesia was gaining far more from the arrangement than the territories to the north. Southern Rhodesia became known to Africans as Bamba Zonke - Take All. Not only was the milking of copper profits severely detrimental to the northern economy, but large grants from Federal funds went to the setting up of new industries in the south. The most irritating instance of this came in 1955, when the Federal Government announced without prior consultation that the new Zambezi hydroelectric power station would be sited at Kariba on the south bank of the river.

All this served to weaken a Federation which was already dying. Its own constitution required that it be reviewed seven to nine years after its formation. The job of conducting the first review fell to Lord Monckton, one of Britain's most distinguished lawyers. To the horror of the Federal Government his report recommended that "the strength of African opposition in the Northern territories is such that the Federation cannot, in our view, be maintained in its present form". In the event, it was dissolved in December 1963 with Northern Rhodesia and Nyasaland only months away from Independence.

The position of the white minority was becoming ever more isolated. At the end of the year, no fewer than eighteen African states had gained full independence and many more were to follow.

In the meantime, opposition to white minority rule had become more focused, and out of the rash of trade unions emerged the Zimbabwe African Peoples Union (ZAPU) under the leadership of a former railwayman called Joshua Nkomo. Ideological schisms within the party eventually caused a split, and on 8 August 1963, the Zimbabwe African National Union (ZANU) was formed with Ndabaninge Sithole as President. Among its members were Leopold Takawira, Enos Nkala, Maurice Nyangumbo – and a bright young firebrand called Robert Mugabe.

By now the settlers had become frightened of convulsions taking place elsewhere on the continent, and had seen images of white refugees fleeing the newly independent state of Zaire. But the British refused to give them what they asked for: any independence had to be conditional on the acceptance of black majority rule at some stage in the future.

This notion was, in fact, acceptable to a minority of the settler community. Their government had endorsed the new constitution proposed by Britain in 1961. The concession to black demands had been a small one, but even this proved too much for the majority of whites in Rhodesia at that time. The government took a step to the right in April 1964 when the Prime Minister, Winston Field, was replaced by Ian Smith.

Relations with Britain got worse until finally, on 11 November 1965, Rhodesia announced its own Unilateral Declaration of Independence.

THE UDI YEARS

Although it was rather a blow to Britain's standing in the world, the rebellion was met with the feeblest of protest from London. For Rhodesian whites, the sanctions were little more than an inconvenience. There was a scarcity of luxury goods, but employment was hardly affected, and if the whites did suffer any fall in living standards, for most it was from a position of such affluence that it could be accommodated with ease. By 1972, the level of exports had actually risen higher than when UDI was declared. Not only did foreign tourists keep on coming but so too did more white immigrants.

For the Africans, the armed struggle began in earnest on 28 April 1966, when seven guerrillas of the Zimbabwe National Liberation Army (ZANLA), the military wing of ZANU, were killed in what is now called the Battle of Chinoyhi. Over the next three years ZANLA and the Zimbabwe People's Revolutionary Army (ZIPRA), the military wing of ZAPU, fought a number of battles against the Rhodesian forces, but they were not able to match the superior weaponry available to the government troops. They were further hampered by the fact that they were forced to operate from outside the country's borders, in Zambia and Tanzania.

Diplomatically, the early years of UDI were good to Ian Smith. In 1966 and 1968, he had a series of talks with Britain which enabled him to come away with almost everything he wanted. A touch of the bizarre was added to the negotiations in the way they were conducted: aboard British naval ships which sailed in circles in the Mediterranean Sea.

Back home, Smith introduced a new constitution for Rhodesia, designed to keep power permanently in white hands. The constitution of 1969, in Smith's own words, "sounded the death knell of the notion of majority rule". It was overwhelmingly endorsed by referendum, few blacks being entitled to vote.

Matters were made worse for the liberation movement when, two years later, Britain endorsed a settlement based on this constitution. The British Foreign Secretary, Sir Alec Douglas-Home, agreed to lift sanctions and allow the 1969 constitution to remain in place with little by way of amendments. Not only was there no provision for the lifting of racist laws but there were no safeguards to prevent Smith from altering the constitution further in his favour at a later date. Smith's main concession was to accept the principle that one day majority rule would come, but the system was so devised that in real terms it would take generations. The white population was jubilant at Smith's achievement and relieved at the end of their isolation from the world. In London, shares with Rhodesian interest had millions of pounds added to their value within minutes.

All that was left for Smith was to test the settlement on the country's entire population, a condition he had long agreed with the British. He was optimistic that such a test would be a mere formality, describing the black population as "the happiest Africans in the world". As for the liberation parties, they were gloomy at the prospects of getting the settlement defeated. The nationalist parties were banned and their leaders, Ndabaningi Sithole and Joshua Nkomo were both languishing in detention. With those two safely out of the way there was just enough in the agreement to satisfy the broad mass of the African population - or so the theory went.

The test of acceptability was due to start at the beginning of 1972. With just four weeks to go a new nationalist organisation, the African National Council (ANC), was formed under the leadership of an unassuming bishop called Abel Muzorewa. The task ahead was daunting. With little in the way of funds and inadequate offices, the ANC had to take on a well-equipped propaganda machine, with all the apparatus of radio and press at its disposal.

In the event, the ANC's campaign surprised everyone. For the first time since Europeans set foot in the country the African people of Rhodesia were being consulted about their future. The effect was almost magical. By the time a team of British commissioners arrived in Rhodesia to supervise the referendum, an astonishing groundswell of resentment had built up. The commissioners were overwhelmed by expressions of misgiving about the constitution and mistrust of Smith's government. Smith countered by claiming that the people had been the victims of intimidation by the ANC. After two months Lord Pearce, the head of the commission, withdrew to consider his verdict. In May 1972, Sir Alec Douglas Home received it. "In our opinion," Pearce had written, "the people of Rhodesia as a whole do not regard the proposals as acceptable as a basis for independence."

The conclusion marked a turning point in the country's history. On one hand it provided just the catalyst for which the nationalists had been hoping. On the other, it prompted Smith's government to seek revenge by passing a vindictive round of repressive legislation through parliament: tougher pass laws, segregated public facilities and controlled areas for the entry of blacks into urban areas.

Such measures only prompted further resistance. By December 1972, ZANU guerrillas were ready to launch their next campaign, a carefully planned sequence of attacks on isolated, unarmed white farmsteads in the east of the country. Unlike the assaults of the sixties which came from across the Zambezi in the north, an attack from the east had the advantage of mountainous terrain which provided good cover for effective guerrilla activity. But perhaps more important than either of these factors was the extent of local support which the guerrillas now enjoyed.

The Rhodesians were only too aware of this. Accordingly, government officers were given wide powers to impose heavy fines on any African villager suspected of helping rebels. Cattle were often seized in lieu of money. In the area closest to the border, thousands were removed from their villages to facilitate army retaliation. Later, thousands more were placed in protected villages in an effort to deprive guerrillas of local support.

These countermeasures were effective, but the guerrilla threat was never destroyed and the war, though highly localised, had an effect which rippled throughout the country. Defence expenditure rocketed and the economy suffered badly from the prolonged periods in which white employees had to serve in the security services. Whites began to leave the country. Eventually, Smith was forced to start talking with the Bishop. Beginning in July 1973, the negotiations dragged on for ten desultory months, achieving little.

But Smith was not able to play for time much longer. He may have hoped that the offensive would eventually peter out, but a coup d'état in a country thousands of miles away was to affect his fortunes radically. In April 1974, the downfall of the Salazar government in Lisbon brought an abrupt end to Portuguese rule in Mozambique. At a stroke, Rhodesia's entire eastern border – over a thousand kilometres of it – became a front which had to be protected from guerrilla attack. At the same time, the South African premier, John Vorster, calculated that with Mozambique no longer sympathetic he would rather see a stable black government dependent on his good will than an unstable white one which was continually draining his resources.

Having supported Smith openly in his rebellion, Vorster now adopted a subtle change of tack, designed to force him to accommodate the nationalists. He found an unlikely ally in President Kenneth Kaunda of Zambia, who was becoming increasingly concerned at the effect which the war was having in his own country. Meeting in secret, Vorster and Kaunda devised an elaborate scheme to bring Smith to the table with a united front of nationalist leaders. The plan was not destined to be a success. Nationalist unity was forestalled by a flurry of internal dissension, during which one prominent guerrilla leader, Herbert Chitepo, lost his life in a car bomb attack. By the time a conference was arranged, neither side was convinced that it could serve much purpose. The meeting eventually took place. In what was becoming a tradition for interesting summit venues, this one took place on a train parked on the bridge which spans the Zambezi at Victoria Falls. But despite the presence of the Zambian and South African premiers, it broke up in a matter of hours.

The scheme, though bizarre and unlikely from the outset, had a marked effect on future events. For, in order to take place at all, the conference had necessitated the release from gaol of three crucial nationalist leaders - Nkomo, Sithole and Mugabe. It was Mugabe's star which was now in the ascendant. The most militant of the three, he believed firmly that only war would bring down the Rhodesian government, and once he was free he lost no time in organising a recruitment campaign for ZANU's guerrilla army. Thousands were dispatched across the border into Mozambique, to be joined by Mugabe himself in April 1975.

Nkomo's ZAPU guerrillas joined Mugabe's forces in a new campaign of disruption. White farms were attacked, stores were robbed and land mines were planted. With ZANU operating from Mozambique and ZAPU from Zambia the minority government found itself fighting a battle on two fronts. Now, every able-bodied man under the age of thirty-eight was liable for military service, to the consequent detriment of the economy.

Inevitably, the war in Rhodesia was attracting worldwide attention. Fear of a communist takeover prompted the US Secretary of State, Henry Kissinger, to offer Smith a five-point plan which would lead to black majority rule within two years, albeit with whites playing a major role in the drafting of the new constitution. It was a package that immediately ran into trouble. The nationalists within the country had not been consulted, and many were prepared to argue that they were better off resolving the issue by force alone.

By mid-1977, the war had spread right across the country. Guerrilla raids were being made at will in the central towns of Que Que, Gwelo and Shangani. By July, three hundred schools had been forced to close. Mission hospitals and clinics also suffered while African councillors, fearing guerrilla intimidation, refused to participate in the administration of their districts. Smith was resigned to the fact that any solution to the conflict hinged on black majority rule, but he was still hoping for a deal which would maintain a disproportionate role for the whites in the running of the country. In a bid for an internal settlement he opened negotiations with three black leaders whom he considered moderate enough to accede to most of his demands. The three he chose were Abel Muzorewa, who was still popular as the leader of the ANC, Ndabaningi Sithole, whose support as a ZANU leader had withered but still retained credibility, and Jeremiah Chirau, a tribal chief who had at the government's instigation set up a conservative black party within the country.

This combination gave Smith the softest touch he could possibly ask for, and in March 1978, he announced an agreement in which whites occupied twenty eight seats in a parliament of a hundred, together with extensive white control over the administration and security forces. A coalition government was set up, aimed at implementing the terms of the agreement, but it made little headway. Muzorewa's performance in particular had been a disappointment, notably in the black suburbs of Salisbury where his support had traditionally been strong. Not only did the guerrillas refuse to accept an amnesty but progress in implementing reforms favourable to the black population was painfully slow.

For Smith, the main hope of saving the settlement was to test its approval by the people. He set up an election, scheduled for April 1979. This was to become a trial of strength for the government, who exhorted Africans to vote, and the guerrillas, who tried to stop them. By mobilising as many white men as he could, Smith afforded massive protection at the polling stations, with the result that the turnout was impressively high. The clear winner was Muzorewa, with seventy per cent of the votes polled. Thus, on 31 May 1979, nearly a century after Cecil Rhodes first set foot north of the Limpopo, white rule finally came to an end.

The anti-climax was deafening. There was no great public ceremony, no new flag, and no dancing in the streets. While the poll must, under the circumstances, have been as accurate a reflection of the people's wishes as could be measured, a war-weary electorate had simply voted for a black leader who could offer them peace. Much of the machinery of government was still in white hands, and they knew it. The very presence of Smith as a minister simply reinforced that impression. Even the name 'Rhodesia' was retained in the republic's new title - henceforth it was to be known as 'Zimbabwe-Rhodesia'.

More important still was the fact that ZANU and ZAPU had both been excluded from taking part in the election, thus depriving any new government of vital intellectual power. Few in the international community were satisfied that a new nation had been born, and many sanctions remained in place.

THE CARRINGTON FACTOR

Once again, it appeared that the conflict would drag on without an end in sight. But once again another foreign change of government was to have a decisive effect on the future of the country. In May 1979, Britain elected its Conservative Party into office under the leadership of Margaret

Thatcher. It was not the Prime Minister herself but one of her ministers who was to make the headway now. Lord Carrington, the new Foreign Secretary, persuaded her that to recognise Muzorewa's government would simply alienate African and Commonwealth states, and perpetuate the war. Carrington decided to grasp the nettle which successive British governments had left well alone since UDI in 1965 - accept full responsibility as the former colonial authority for a complete and orderly transfer of power. The first stage was to draw up a new constitution and present it at a conference to which both Muzorewa and the Patriotic Front would be invited. This constitution would drastically reduce the disproportionate white influence which Muzorewa had been prepared to accept.

The conference opened at Lancaster House in London in September 1979. In attendance were Muzorewa, Smith, Nkomo and Mugabe. Against all expectations the talks, which went on for fourteen weeks, proved to be a success.

Under the terms of the agreement a British governor, Lord Soames, was dispatched to Salisbury armed with full executive and legislative powers to manage a transition to Independence and supervise the first elections. In spite of intimidation from vested interests on all sides, the cease-fire held up well enough to allow orderly voting to take place. The election was seen essentially as a contest between two men, Abel Muzorewa and Robert Mugabe, with Nkomo not expected to show spectacular support.

On the strength of his showing in 1979, it was thought that Muzorewa would at least gain enough seats to lead an alliance which included both the whites and Nkomo. In the event, the election results, announced on March 4th, 1980, proved an overwhelming victory for Mugabe. Of the eighty black seats which were now available in parliament, Mugabe took fifty-seven, Nkomo twenty, and Muzorewa only three.

For the white minority, the result appeared the worst of all possible worlds. Mugabe had been portrayed to them as the most rabid black leader of them all, an uncompromising radical who made no secret of his Marxist sympathies. In despair, many of them prepared to leave the country and start new homes abroad.

But the biggest surprise of all awaited them. That night, Mugabe made his inaugural television broadcast. In it, he declared simply and concisely that "...there is a place for everyone in this country. We want to ensure a sense of security for both the winners and the losers." In the space of a few minutes, the scales fell from the eyes of thousands of white Rhodesians. The voice they heard was not that of the half-crazed ogre they had feared. This was not the ranting of an "apostle of Satan" as Ian Smith had once described him. Instead it was a voice of sobriety and conciliation. It was this broadcast, as much as the election which preceded it, which was to mould the future of the country. In it Mugabe laid bare the foundations of the new republic for all to see: a world in which black and white would live and work together, towards the common goal of peace and prosperity for all.

That night, over a month before the official day of Independence, the Republic of Zimbabwe was born.

INDEPENDENCE

On March 11th, Lord Soames summoned Mugabe to form a government as Prime Minister. Canaan Banana, an American-educated Methodist clergyman, who had been leader of Mugabe's internal organisation, was elected President on April 11th by a joint session of the legislature. A week later, on April 18th, the British flag was hauled down in Salisbury in ceremonies which marked formally the independence of Zimbabwe.

There was still a sense of unease when, on that day, the Prince of Wales handed the instruments of power to the new government. A wrong move by anyone could so easily have upset the delicate balance which had now been achieved.

Quite apart from their material situation it was very hard for many of these people to make the psychological adjustment to the new order. Many of the younger ones had grown up knowing little other than a life of violence and subterfuge, and the task of convincing them that they could now come in from the bush was never going to be an easy one.

Although Mugabe had always been perceived as the most radical of the leaders in the Independence struggle, there was a less radical restructuring of the social order than many had anticipated. Whites were, of course, divested of ultimate political power, although they still had a formal role in the government and sometimes a good deal to say in its day-to-day operations. In a move that was both pragmatic and conciliatory, Mugabe made a point of inviting them to stay on and help build the country as Zimbabweans. Many were encouraged by Mugabe's moderation, but others felt frustrated by the economic adjustments the government made, by the inflammatory statements of some government leaders, and by the general influx of Africans into positions of power. In the two years after Independence nearly a quarter of the white population left the country - mostly to South Africa.

In foreign policy, the government courted socialist allies. Every member of the Warsaw Pact established relations with the new 'fraternal' African ally, opening embassies and peopling them with trade commissioners, cultural attachés and journalists. Solidarity was marked by cultural tours by East European acrobats, pianists, artists and ballet troupes while, occasionally, leaders would pay state visits, none more cynical than that of Nicolae Ceaucescu of Romania, who made it clear from the moment he arrived that he wanted no more than to shoot an elephant and head back home.

But there was one non-socialist country with which the new republic was bound to retain strong links. Despite an intense dislike for apartheid, Mugabe realised that his country's economy and security were largely dependent on the Republic of South Africa. On becoming Prime Minister, he maintained economic co-operation while refusing official diplomatic relations, a policy which may have proved hard for some to swallow but which was dictated by circumstance.

The government's control over sporadic violence at home was limited in part because about a third of the guerrillas had been ZIPRA fighters loyal to Joshua Nkomo. Moreover, Mugabe's power over his own ZANLA troops was limited by the fact that during the war successful guerrilla tactics had placed little emphasis on troop discipline and gave a great deal of autonomy to soldiers in the field.

The prime minister, admitting that "no-one is blameless, least of all elements within my own party," came to rely on the police and military forces he had inherited from the previous government, but only when other attempts to control the guerrillas had failed. In October 1980, Mugabe finally cracked down by sending troops from the national army into rural trouble spots and by reinforcing police patrols in the cities. At the same time, the integration into the national army of most of the remaining 50,000 guerrillas brought most of the civil violence to an end.

But it was not simply young blacks who had been responsible for upsetting the delicate constitution of the new republic. Several acts of sabotage, including one on the ZANU PF headquarters in the capital, were directly attributable to disgruntled, South Africa-backed whites, and there was at least one occasion when the overthrow of the government was being seriously contemplated in white circles.

ETHNICITY - THE AGE-OLD PROBLEM

It was just two years after Zimbabwe's Independence that the ethnic divisions, which had been latent throughout the civil war, came to the surface. The rivalry between ZANU and ZAPU had never been purely political. ZANU, which had operated from Mozambique, into Shona-populated areas of east and north-east Zimbabwe, appealed to Shona ethnicity as a tactical necessity in building ties with the local population. On the other hand, ZAPU garnered the loyalties of the Ndebele, not least because that was the ethnic origin of Joshua Nkomo. The Kalanga, a group ethnically classed as Shona, but politically aligned to the Ndebele, was also more sympathetic to ZAPU.

The post war conflict, now about to take place, was the result of mutual suspicion between the parties. ZANU-PF members, many of whom wanted Zimbabwe to become a one party state, suspected PF-ZAPU's desire to retain a separate identity within the country's ruling coalition. At the same time, many Ndebele feared Shona dominance from ZANU-PF's political power. In February 1981, some three hundred former guerrillas were killed after fighting at a bar in a Bulawayo army camp escalated into serious inter-factional violence. Government officials and ZAPU leaders called for a halt in the fighting, and order was restored within a few days. The battalions responsible were promptly dissolved, and most of the combatants were eventually integrated into other units.

The next serious disturbance came in February 1982 when large quantities of arms and equipment were found by the Central Intelligence Organisation cached on farms owned by companies controlled by ZAPU. Not only were scores of military vehicles uncovered, but also communications equipment, SAM-7 surface-to-air missiles, hundreds of machine guns, rocket launchers, mortars, anti-aircraft guns, several thousand automatic rifles and ammunition. Mugabe charged that Nkomo and elements within ZAPU had been planning a coup against his government. Within days, Nkomo and three other ZAPU ministers and deputy ministers were outlawed and their assets confiscated.

In the wake of this humiliation, and the murders of ZAPU combatants in integrated army camps, Ndebele dissidence increased. Thousands deserted from the armed forces, and by the middle of 1982 a large proportion of them were operating as guerrillas in the bush in the west and south west of the country. Moving around in bands of a dozen or so, the dissidents resorted to banditry. A group of them kidnapped six foreign tourists in July 1982, prompting a national manhunt. The dissidents said they would release their victims only in return for the release of the jailed ZIPRA leaders and the end of government harassment of Nkomo. In the event, the victims were murdered. Mugabe's government acted sternly against the rebels, making sweeps through guerrilla areas, uncovering several caches of arms and arresting dissidents. The wave of repression intensified when the North Korean-trained Fifth Brigade was sent in to flush out remaining dissidents. Some report that thousands of civilians were killed in the process.

Such actions only served to strengthen ZAPU support in Matabeleland, and the government realised the dangers of a tactic which might play into the hands of South Africa, which had developed a fondness for attempting to destabilise the fledgling republic. Mugabe, ever the pragmatist, could see the danger signs. He assured Nkomo, who had fled to Britain, that he would be safe to return in order that a settlement could be negotiated.

On 22 December 1987, the two parties merged, although some felt that it was more a case of ZANU absorbing the opposition. Nkomo was given a senior position and Mugabe, who had hitherto been Prime Minister, assumed the role of President. By May 1988, the dissidents had given themselves up under an amnesty, and the sporadic attacks dried up.

Since then, fears that a one party state would close the door on democratic traditions have proved largely groundless. Newspapers in particular have exposed scandals in government and industry without suffering closure. The University of Zimbabwe has been the source of strident anti-government criticism but, although it has been closed on occasion, it continues to function, albeit now under State control.

The service sectors of the economy have seen vast improvements. In education, primary and secondary schools have expanded from a total pre-Independence capacity of under a million to well over three million in 1990. The university intake is now ten thousand - ten times greater than it was in 1979 - and universities in Bulawayo and Mutare are now being built. The health services have seen a total restructuring, with new hospitals and clinics springing up in every province. In keeping with the World Health Organisation's ideal of 'Health for all by the year 2,000', great emphasis has been laid on primary health care, with hundreds of primary health care facilities being constructed in areas which had been poorly served before 1980. An extensive water supply infrastructure has also been built up through the use of boreholes, rural dams and pipe-borne water to villages.

But despite the availability of all these services, as well as the diversity of the industrial and agricultural base, the Zimbabwean economy is not without its difficulties. Recent years have seen limited growth with rapid inflation, falling investment and rising unemployment. Heavy external debts and shortages of foreign exchange have all taken their toll.

One of the country's gravest crises came in 1992, when the worst drought in living memory led to acute human suffering and the death of thousands of animals. Power cuts disrupted city life, while in the rural areas, poorer people were reduced to eating leaves and berries. The government came under heavy fire for failing to heed advance warnings of a maize shortage, but the absence of truly convincing political opposition saved the day for ZANU.

Apart from the vagaries of the regional climate, another factor is likely to complicate Zimbabwe's economic fortunes still further in the future. Ever since President de Klerk embarked on the precarious business of dismantling apartheid, South Africa has been drawn inexorably back into the international community. De Klerk and his party's old adversary, Nelson Mandela, are now Nobel Laureates for the work they have done, and one effect of their protracted negotiations has been to restore the acceptability of South Africa's trade with the outside world. With a much bigger infrastructure, Zimbabwe's southern neighbour is in a position to provide blistering competition in all sectors of the economy, from mining to tourism. Better perks and working conditions also threaten to lure many of Zimbabwe's professionals to seek their fortunes in Cape Town, Durban and Johannesburg rather than the commercial centres of their homeland.

In particular, tourism throughout the region is rapidly expanding. Not only South Africa, but Botswana and Namibia are all very attractive to affluent visitors from the northern hemisphere. These nations represent both a threat and an opportunity for Zimbabwe: on one hand, they all have singular attractions within their own borders, but at the same time they offer the possibility of holidays in more than one country, thus enhancing international interest in the region.

Zimbabwe's immediate preoccupation is to cope with the Structural Adjustment Programme, developed with the World Bank and International Monetary Fund, aimed to take full advantage of Zimbabwe's strengths and correct the economy's inherent weaknesses. The plan essentially opens up the country to imports, improves incentives for investors and devalues the local currency. But for most Zimbabweans, this involves two painful prescriptions: reductions in government spending and the cutting of subsidies on food products.

These policies have had a wide range of effects, including a serious erosion in the quality of state health care and other public facilities. The devaluation of the Zimbabwe dollar has fuelled domestic inflation, a factor which, together with the removal of subsidies on certain basic foodstuffs, has made life hard for the poor. Some observers are openly cynical about the whole operation, claiming that the World Bank's real agenda is debt repayment rather than the advertised 'short term belt tightening for long term gain'.

At the end of the day, Zimbabwe needs to find ways of boosting manufacturing output in order to reduce its dependence on the export of primary products like tobacco, gold and cotton, which are vulnerable to wide fluctuations in price. New investment does not need simply to expand existing industries but to introduce modern technology in order to lessen the nation's dependence on the outside world for machinery. Thus the country would reduce its expenditure of foreign exchange while at the same time enlarging its capacity for earning it by increasing its export of manufactured goods.

The challenge is a tough one, but Zimbabwe is better placed than most African countries to meet it. Not only is there a spectacularly wide variety of resources at its disposal, but a skilled local labour force is available to exploit it. The pictures which follow represent the most ambitious attempt yet to document the diversity of activities to be found within Zimbabwe's borders. While it may be a land of gorgeous scenery and exotic wildlife, it is far more important to record it as a nation of people, for they, too, have their story.

ZIMBABWE'S HERITAGE

It will not be long before a whole generation has grown up with no direct recollection of what Zimbabwe was like before Independence. Both within the country and abroad, a new set of images, quite divorced from the memories of guerrilla warfare and political infighting, is slowly establishing itself in the minds of those with an interest in the country. As the end of the century approaches, what do visitors to Zimbabwe want to see, and what can they expect to gain from the experience?

Without doubt, two outstanding features of the country's heritage are known throughout the world. One is its huge and varied portfolio of archaeological sites. Great Zimbabwe itself was the hub of a powerful pre-colonial empire, but there are dozens of smaller ruins, as well as hundreds of prehistoric cave paintings scattered across the country. The other is the largest curtain of falling water anywhere in the world, created by the Zambezi River as it plunges into a succession of deep gorges in the earth's crust - the Victoria Falls.

Zimbabwe would be worth a fortnight of anyone's life if only to see these marvels, yet they constitute a fraction of all that the country has to offer. The purpose of this book is to illustrate the full diversity of Zimbabwe as never before, depicting every aspect of its natural resources and social life. But before picking our way through the dozens of attractions awaiting the discerning tourist, we have devoted this first chapter to those for which the country is most obviously famous. Even here, there is more to savour than initial impressions suggest.

BEGINNINGS

Zimbabweans take great pride in the abundant evidence of ancient civilisation within their borders. Scattered from one end of the country to the other are stone ruins and rock paintings which betray not one but several pre-colonial cultures. The most celebrated site of all is the huge archipelago of walled structures known as Great Zimbabwe, a shrine of such ideological importance that it is widely used as a symbol for the nation. One of its most famous sculptures, a stone bird, is the badge of Zimbabwe, and can be seen on the nation's flag, medals and coins. The Conical Tower is reproduced on stamps and bank notes, not to mention countless postcards and books which are seen all over the world.

But Great Zimbabwe is unique only in its size. Of the many smaller sites, some demonstrate a greater aesthetic sense and superior technology, though they are hardly mentioned in many text books or tourist brochures. Knowledge of their existence is vital, for they are proof of a far more extensive civilisation than Great Zimbabwe alone represents. Moreover, these ruins are by no means the earliest evidence of human activity in the region. Many of the paintings on rocks and cave walls are more than thirty thousand years old.

Visitors to Great Zimbabwe are often surprised by the size and the area covered by this ancient site.

Who were the first Zimbabweans? In purely genetic terms, they were hardly different from the first Indians, Orientals or Europeans. In the first few million years after a group of apes began standing upright, Africa and Asia were inhabited by several forms of early man, most of whom became extinct. By the late Stone Age, only one type, Homo Sapiens, survived. Unlike his predecessors he was an organised, social animal, mastering the art of making tools for hunting and constructing shelters. Later he developed an aesthetic sense, interpreting his environment in rock paintings.

The artists who did this were known as the San, a late Stone Age hunter-gatherer people. The natural abundance of iron gave them ferrous pigments which yielded a wide variety of yellows, reds and browns, as well as white and black. Their pictures often took the form of large friezes covering the walls of rock shelters, some representing complex religious preoccupations as well as the rituals of daily survival. The paintings visible today depict mythical creatures, wild animals, men hunting and families in their camps – even the odd scene of domestic violence.

The cultural development of Zimbabwe took a great leap forward with the smelting of iron. The first Iron Age people are thought to have crossed the Zambezi from the north about two thousand years ago, and the technology they brought with them was revolutionary. With them came the manufacture of metal tools and weapons, organised agriculture, and larger settlements based on more sophisticated building techniques. By the tenth century after Christ, a distinctive culture began to emerge, with its own language and patterns of social exchange. The existing trade system was developed dramatically, especially with the Muslims who lived along the east coast of the African continent.

By now, the smelting of gold and copper had been perfected as well. These metals, along with ivory and skins, were exchanged for cloth and beads from India and Persia. Even porcelain from China has been found in Zimbabwe's ancient settlements. The trade soon flourished to such an extent that local rulers were able to establish a state system centred at Great Zimbabwe.

These rulers were rich in cattle, and with such an asset their sphere of influence was bound to be extensive. Before long, the Shona people had acquired wealth exceeding that of any other group in the interior of southern Africa, and by the fourteenth century they had settlements and trading posts extending over many thousands of square kilometres. The city of Great Zimbabwe itself probably contained more than ten thousand people.

Other stone settlements were built throughout the region. Unlike the cathedrals of Europe or the mosques of the Arab world they did not have to support heavy roofing, so there were fewer constraints on the way in which the masonry could be organised. The walls were not geometric in their design, but flowed with the contours of the hills and granite rocks. There was no mortar, so the bricks could slip against one another as the earth subsided beneath their weight. The effectiveness of the stonework is borne out by the amount that is still standing after several centuries, without any cement to hold it together.

Wherever outcrops of good building rock were found next to grazing land, more of these settlements were built, some becoming great trade centres in their own right. The social structure in these towns was such that many dwellers could be freed from the mechanics of daily survival to become skilled potters, weavers and metal workers. Each town would also have an army to guard its herds and defend the local mines.

There were two major constraints which prevented this unique civilisation from developing still further. Firstly, they did not have the wheel, so in the absence of horses it was impossible for a city to depend on grazing lands beyond walking distance. Secondly, they had no written word, so there was a limit to the complexity of the administration which could be effected.

By the fifteenth century Great Zimbabwe was no longer able to sustain itself, and slowly the city died. At some stage the supply of crops, firewood, game and grazing would have been outstripped by demand, and by 1500 AD the settlement was in total decay. Quite how the system collapsed is unclear, but it is likely that the local environment could no longer support such a large population.

But the skills which had been mastered lived on. As Great Zimbabwe declined the younger city of Khami, three hundred kilometres to the west, began to flourish. Over the next two hundred years, other smaller settlements were built, forming the larger, single state of Torwa. The ruins at Dhlo Dhlo and Naletale exhibit much more intricate stonework than that which had gone before, and artifacts found at these sites reveal contact with the early Portuguese traders.

By the late nineteenth century, the damage done by civil war and European excesses destroyed much of the material evidence for Zimbabwe's original culture. At the time, racial prejudice was such that many of the white arrivals who saw the stonework at Great Zimbabwe itself were quite unable to understand how it could have been produced by local people. Elaborate theories were constructed which attributed the ruins to Phoenicians, Arabs and other outsiders. Such myths were finally laid to rest in 1932 when Gertrude Caton-Thompson, a highly respected archaeologist, was requested to investigate the site. Her detailed excavations proved beyond doubt that Great Zimbabwe was the work of indigenous Shona craftsmen.

Evidence of a distinctive culture within the borders of modern Zimbabwe can be traced as far back as 30,000 years. The country's ancient rock art enjoys a world-wide reputation and illustrates the close relationship which prehistoric Africans established with the animal kingdom. Buffalo, zebra, kudu, elephant and rhino are all depicted in abundance, as well as early hunters and farmers. Most of the rock paintings visible today were executed between one and five thousand years ago, but have been remarkably well preserved in the dry air of the African bush. Outcrops of rock like the one below near the Save river in the Eastern Highlands, occur all over the country. The caves within such slabs were the main form of refuge for prehistoric Zimbabweans.

Great Zimbabwe is the largest ancient construction in sub-Saharan Africa. The wall around the Great Enclosure is over 250 metres long and uses 15,000 tonnes of carefully hewn rock. Modern dating techniques indicate that building on this site began around 1200 AD. The city is thought to have reached the height of its wealth and importance some hundred and fifty years later, before it declined to insignificance by the sixteenth century. The most striking single edifice within the ruins is the Conical Tower, which stands at the heart of the Great Enclosure surrounded by trees. The fact that it is solid suggests that it had no functional value but was built for symbolic or sacred reasons. It is thought to represent a Shona grain silo.

Massive as they are, the stone walls are most
unlikely to have supported any kind of roof. Instead
they formed circular enclosures, with houses built
inside. Evidence found on the site indicates that the
people who constructed Great Zimbabwe were also
skilled workers in iron, copper, gold and clay. Cattle,
however, were the mainstay of the economy. The
ruins, impressive though they may be, are just
a skeleton: what they must have looked like when
adorned with painted clay, carved wood, beaten
metal, thatch and brightly-dyed cloth must be
left to the imagination.

Great Zimbabwe carries great emotional
significance to the people of the modern republic,
for it is the most powerful evidence of pre-colonial
culture to be found in southern Africa. The very
name 'Zimbabwe' is taken from this monument.

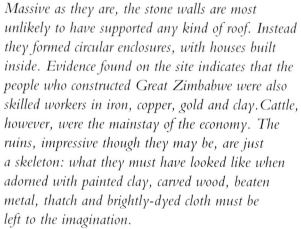

Standing on an outcrop which overlooks the Great
Enclosure is the Hill Complex, a labyrinth of rooms
and passages open to the sky. Conservationists
regularly monitor the masonry for any kind
of movement in order that remedial action can be
taken if the foundations start to slip. Certain
segments of the walls are in danger of collapse
because erosion and the movement of tree roots
are causing the ground to shift.

A technician from the University of Zimbabwe examines a reconstruction of the masonry from the Great Enclosure, in an attempt to understand how the dry stone walling has remained standing for so long. The University is playing a very active role in conserving the site.

Great Zimbabwe may be the biggest, but in Midlands Province the younger ruins at Regina, Dhlo Dhlo (Danangombe) and Nalatale all demonstrate more intricate craftsmanship than their predecessor.

Artifacts discovered at these sites also reveal extensive contact with the outside world. At Dhlo Dhlo, a Portuguese cannon has been found, as well as fragments of Ming pottery from China.

Further west still is the old Torwa capital, Khami, (right) a short drive from Bulawayo.

THE VICTORIA FALLS

The Victoria Falls constitute one of the most spectacular natural wonders of the world. Here in the far north-west of the country, the Zambezi River flows, broad and placid, to the brink of a basalt lip seventeen hundred metres wide, before taking a headlong plunge of one hundred metres into the frothy chasm of the gorge below. Long before David Livingstone encountered the Falls in 1856, they were known as Mosi-Oa-Tunya, 'the smoke that thunders', undoubtedly because the spray sent shooting into the sky can be seen from several hours' walk away.

The flow of water varies greatly according to the time of the year and the intensity of the rains in the upper tributaries of the Zambezi. At the end of a normal rainy season in March or April, the volume going over the Falls in one minute is around half a million cubic metres, but in the dry season in December it can be less than a twentieth of this. The best time to see the Falls is probably half way between these two extremes. But they are still spectacular when not in full flood, because they are not obscured at close quarters by the opacity of the spray.

Livingstone himself believed that the Falls had been caused by some great rupture of the earth's crust in the distant past. Geological evidence now indicates that the present chasm is the eighth in a succession which has worked its way upstream over several million years. From a nearby airstrip, light aircraft regularly take tourists over the lip of the Falls themselves, to provide a vantage point from which the landscape betrays this story with crystal clarity.

But there is far more to do at Victoria Falls than to marvel at the Falls alone. Upstream, the Zambezi plays host to the famous 'sundowner' cruises, champagne-fuelled excursions onto the river to watch the wildlife from the nearby National Park. For those with the courage, there is a very different experience to be had: the rapids immediately downstream offer some of the most terrifying white water rafting anywhere in the world.

There is also a spectacular excursion to be made on foot. Overlooking the eighth chasm opposite the Falls is the Rain Forest, a mass of dense tropical vegetation which thrives on the unique conditions created by the spray from the Falls themselves. Winding its way through the sodden branches is a footpath, with occasional diversions to viewing points for those unhampered by vertigo.

Immediately to the south of the Victoria Falls is the town of the same name, an attractive settlement founded at the beginning of the century when there was first talk of harnessing the Zambezi for hydro-electric power. Today its lifeblood is tourism, the streets offering all manner of diversions from shops offering local carvings to safaris into the nearby national park. Although visitors come here from all over the world, Victoria Falls has remained small and accessible, and the town is happily devoid of the hamburger joints and discotheques which have internationalised so many other tourist centres around the world.

Nonetheless, there are some excellent hotel facilities: the famous Victoria Falls Hotel was built in 1904, and is still compulsively romantic, an opulent building in the grandest of colonial styles. It occupies a prime site from which the Falls can be seen - and heard - all the year round. Further upstream is Elephant Hills, a much more recent creation which also boasts superb conference facilities. Among other places to stay, the A 'Zambezi Lodge boasts one of the largest thatched roof structures in Africa. The National Park's cottages on the banks of the Zambezi itself offer exceptional value for money.

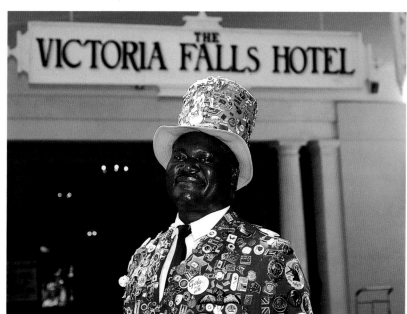

The Victoria Falls are surrounded by a National Park which isolates them from the excesses of modern civilisation. A few minutes' walk from the Livingstone statue is a baobab tree which bears his signature. This particular specimen is thought to be over a thousand years old. Tourists have changed a lot since the days when they were transported to the Falls from the station on trolleys. The pith helmet, so often seen as the clichéd attire of the country's former colonial masters, has now become a practical fashion accessory.

The Victoria Falls are a fine demonstration of how to encourage tourists without damaging the integrity of the very site they have come to see. High rise blocks, discotheques and hamburger joints have all been kept at a discreet distance.

The volume of water falling into the gorge varies greatly according to the time of the year. In November and December after the dry season the flow can be little more than a trickle, but once the rains have come to an end around April, the Falls can be rendered almost invisible by the volume of spray which is kicked up as the water hits the rocks a hundred metres below.

The rapids immediately downstream of the Falls offer some of the best white water rafting in the world. A group of adventurous Americans from Angels Camp in California were the first to negotiate this route in the late 1980s. Since then the company they formed, Sobek, has taken thousands of visitors on one and two-day trips down this stretch of the Zambezi.

For the more adventurous, there is a seven-day trip, which makes the 128 kilometre journey all the way to the mouth of Lake Kariba. Several companies are now offering a similar experience; there is even one offering bungee jumping from the bridge which spans the gorge.

The Rain Forest on the lip of the chasm opposite the Falls is a unique swathe of dense tropical vegetation which thrives in the spray thrown up all year round.

The Victoria Falls bridge was built in 1905. It has a main arch span of 152 metres and is a remarkable feat of engineering even by today's standards.

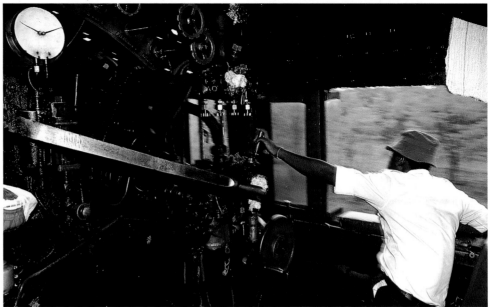

Most countries have long shed their fleets of steam locomotives. Such is the nostalgic value of steam that enthusiasts come from all over the world for the sole purpose of travelling on these trains, which commonly run from Bulawayo to Victoria Falls. Steam trains are still active on other lines but their role is diminishing; the bulk of rail carriage is now by diesel and electric locomotive.

The maintenance of the old steam trains is not easy. Spare parts are no longer available, so have to manufactured from scratch in Bulawayo and Mutare.

THE LURE OF THE CITY LIFE

The cities of Zimbabwe are impressive. Harare, Bulawayo, Gweru, Mutare and a dozen smaller settlements all have something in common – a sense of stability and well-being which makes their atmosphere quite unique in Africa. The streets are much wider than any to be found in Europe and the traffic flows easily. Everywhere there is a cleanliness which puts most international capitals to shame. The shanty towns which bedevil Nairobi, Lagos and Lusaka are conspicuous by their absence. Even the grim, slummy outskirts familiar to Londoners and Parisians are nowhere to be seen. There is, of course, plenty of poverty, but you have to go and look for it. On the other hand the affluent suburbs with their verandas and swimming pools are there for all to see.

In reality, Zimbabweans are essentially a rural people: only one in four lives in a town or city, and very few of these forget their rural roots. The urban businessman, the factory worker, the Member of Parliament and the academic all see their true homes in the country, but their dependence on the cosmopolitan city life is increasing. Go to a bus station at the weekend in any town or city, and the interdependence between urban and rural life is instantly apparent. Buses leaving for the country will have their roof racks laden with goods from the shops and factories of the city, bound for the rural homes and families of their passengers. On the return journeys, the same roof racks are laden with produce from the rural areas, either for sale in the market places or to be consumed during the week. Urban and rural people in Zimbabwe live for each other. Urban areas are the main market for agricultural produce, while at the same time providing jobs and social security for the townspeople who will return to their ancestral homes in old age.

But the tie between town and country is slowly getting looser. As a wider range of professions becomes available in the cities, and as land in the country gets scarcer, a new class of purely urban Africans is emerging, their lives plugged into the world which the international press and satellite television brings before them. Just as most Europeans lost their country roots in the middle of the last century, so will millions of Zimbabweans in the century to come.

Easily the largest of Zimbabwe's urban centres is Harare. It is not only the nation's capital but the most important commercial and industrial centre. The city that grew up around Fort Salisbury bears copious witness to its British heritage. Before Independence, the principal thoroughfares were named after men like Speke, Stanley and Cecil Rhodes himself, although almost all of these have been renamed since. Nonetheless, there are still shopping centres with names like Kensington, Milton Park and Belgravia. Out in the suburbs, orderly English-style gardens with tidy lawns and flower beds, lavender scented shrubberies and ornamental trees are secluded behind neatly trimmed hedges of pink and red hibiscus. Along the broad streets leading to the city centre, the British custom of transplanting the flora of their far-flung colonial possessions lingers in the avenues of flowering jacaranda, red flamboyant and yellow cassias. There's a marked Britishness about the city's sporting venues, too. The Borrowdale racecourse is the centre of the Turf Club of Mashonaland's vast

Now more than a hundred years old, Harare enjoys many different architectural styles. Today the ultra-modern monolith of the Karigamombe Centre dwarfs the Dutch Reformed Church, which was built several generations earlier.

business empire, while other slabs of manicured green are given over to golf, cricket, bowls, tennis, hockey and rugby. But the City's greatest monument to sport must be the National Sports Stadium, with space enough for sixty thousand spectators.

At the very centre of Harare is Unity Square, where in 1890 Colonel Edward Pennefather, Commander of the British Pioneer Column, raised the Union Jack, claiming another piece of Africa for the Empire. Adorned in the middle with a fountain and shaded by enormous trees, the square is bounded by the sharp lines of modern city buildings. The curved monolith of the Monomatapa Hotel dominates the centre of town, eighteen storeys high and squeaky clean. A short stroll away is the still more modern Karigamombe House, a steel and glass construction which belongs firmly in the next century. Out to the west are the Sheraton Hotel and Harare International Conference Centre, whose brassy exteriors combine to make another futuristic building, referred to by locals as 'the Benson and Hedges advert'.

Not all of Harare is so cosmopolitan. Out at Mbare, Graniteside and Highfields there is a much more parochial world of markets where everything from basketwork to love potions are up for sale. The bus station at daybreak is another sight to behold: here at first light comes the army of workers from the surrounding villages. After journeys of two hours and more their collective breath brings a mist to the chill of the African dawn. An hour later the flood is reduced to a trickle, and the army has set about its task of keeping the urban machine running. As the sun goes down, the tide will be moving back out again.

Despite the economic strictures which shackle the country, Harare is still a rapidly expanding city. The original layout was not designed for a burgeoning population, and the proximity of some residential areas to the heart of the city is putting heavy constraints on the expansion of the central business district. Out in the industrial estates beyond the suburbs, new factories are forever extending the city's boundaries, but careful planning is preventing the capital from becoming a hotchpotch. To those who know Cairo, Lagos or Abidjan, Harare is a delight.

If Zimbabwe had achieved statehood without European intervention, it might well have been two countries, so distinct are the Shona and Ndebele people. Harare would have been one capital, Bulawayo the other. Unlike Harare, Bulawayo is built on an African site, the name deriving from an Ndebele word meaning 'The Place of Slaughter'. The Ndebele had always been an aggressive people, and it was chosen to commemorate King Lobengula's many victorious battles.

Today Bulawayo is the second largest city in the country, its appearance bearing many similarities to that of Harare. Laid out on a grid, the streets are even wider than Harare's, originally designed so that a team of sixteen oxen could turn full circle. There are the same handsomely-proportioned buildings, including the most impressive colonial construction in the country. Standing by impeccably maintained lawns and flower gardens, the High Court is a magnificent neoclassical edifice built in 1938, with a copper dome mounted high on a three storey plinth. In the daytime it cuts clean lines against the blue of the sky. Floodlit at night, it is even more spectacular.

Like Harare, Bulawayo is a major industrial centre. Its inhabitants serve the mining and agricultural sectors, as well as a host of manufacturing industries. From the headquarters of Zimbabwe National Railways can be seen the country's principal railway junction, which makes a spectacular sight in itself. Its fleet of more than a hundred steam locomotives was to have been phased out by the end of the 1970s, but the economic constraints on modernisation have ensured their continued viability. Steam trains also stimulate tourism. Thousands of foreign enthusiasts seeking to recapture some vestige of their lost youth come to Bulawayo to admire and travel in the locomotives. The track that runs northwards to Victoria Falls is thought to be the longest straight section of iron rails in the world.

Situated right in the centre of the country is Gweru, Zimbabwe's third city. Despite having a population approaching a quarter of a million people it remains picturesque, with plenty of the old colonial flavour. Gweru was founded in 1894 as a coaching station on the Harare–Bulawayo road, and it rapidly expanded as gold prospectors came to pick over the Great Dyke. But until the 1930s it was principally a farming centre, servicing the beef, dairy and arable holdings which flourish on the local plains. Today, it plays host to gold miners, steel workers and the largest railway marshalling yard in the country.

Tourists find many attractions in the major cities of Zimbabwe, not just sporting amenities but an abundance of museums, restaurants and hotel facilities as well. What they will find harder to reach is the lives of the people. The truth remains that most locals would hardly recognise the Zimbabwe which their foreign benefactors come to see. The price of everyday goods and services often prevents them from enjoying the facilities so readily available to outsiders. This pattern reverberates right across the country: whether in Bulawayo, Mutare, Gweru, Kwekwe or the capital itself, their lives are locked into a different world, symbolised by the crowds which appear each morning, regular as clockwork, at the bus stations.

FOLLOWING PAGE: *Harare in the early morning light. Like all Zimbabwe's major cities it exudes a sense of space and cleanliness unique in Africa.*

The new headquarters of ZANU-PF (right) were completed in 1990. The style of the building is typical of many new blocks now springing up throughout the city. Unlike many of the buildings erected immediately after Independence, this was designed by local architects, Peter Martin and Tony Wales-Smith.

In the heart of the city, First Street (below) is the meeting place for locals and visitors alike. The National Employers' Mutual building on the left dates from 1930 and was the first to be built around a frame of reinforced concrete. It also has one of the earliest clay tile roofs in the city, marking the shift away from corrugated iron which had been previously very popular. Inside the building is the oldest working lift in Harare.

At the turn of the century the very first shops in Harare were built along Manica Road. After Independence, the street was renamed after President Mugabe. The wrought iron railings on the veranda are typical of those to be found on buildings which pre-date the First World War. They were ordered from Britain by catalogue, and fulfiled a useful incidental function as ballast in the holds of ships as they made their way from Scotland to Southern Africa. Once the war came such railings went out of fashion, presumably because the iron was needed to manufacture weapons.

Despite the numerous modern buildings now being built in the centre of Harare, many others have survived from the city's earliest days. In the late twentieth century, pressure of commercial development is posing an increasing threat to their survival.

Cecil House (below) is proof that conservation can be commercially viable. It was restored in 1978, and the newer buildings around it were built in a compatible style.

Harare has the highest concentration of jacaranda trees in the world; throughout September the streets are awash with blossom.

Zimbabwe is one of the few countries in Africa to have an independent judiciary. The Supreme Court (below) represents the pinnacle of the legal system which has evolved from Roman Dutch Law.

Under the Lancaster House agreement, Zimbabwe's Parliament (right) was designed along the Westminster model. The main difference today is that there is a single chamber instead of two.

Although there have been attempts to integrate forms of worship, the established churches in Zimbabwe have evolved a programme of services to satisfy a variety of ethnic constituencies. It is quite common for a church to have one service in English, another for a mixed congregation, and a third in Shona, all in the course of one day.

The University of Zimbabwe is well-equipped with computers. The relaxation of customs regulations at the end of 1990 has made it much easier for this sort of technology to be imported.

The number of A-level students wanting higher education is now so large that the University of Zimbabwe can afford to set a higher entrance requirement than many British universities.

Prince Edward School (below) is one of the oldest and most prestigious in the country. Despite the varied racial mix now evident, the school still sets great store by Victorian values.

Since Independence there has been a dramatic improvement in primary health care facilities throughout the country. The increasing survival rate of infants has resulted in a serious overpopulation problem which is now being addressed by the Ministry of Health. Fortunately the level of literacy in Zimbabwe is higher than that in many African countries, rendering the vigorous family planning programme more effective than elsewhere.

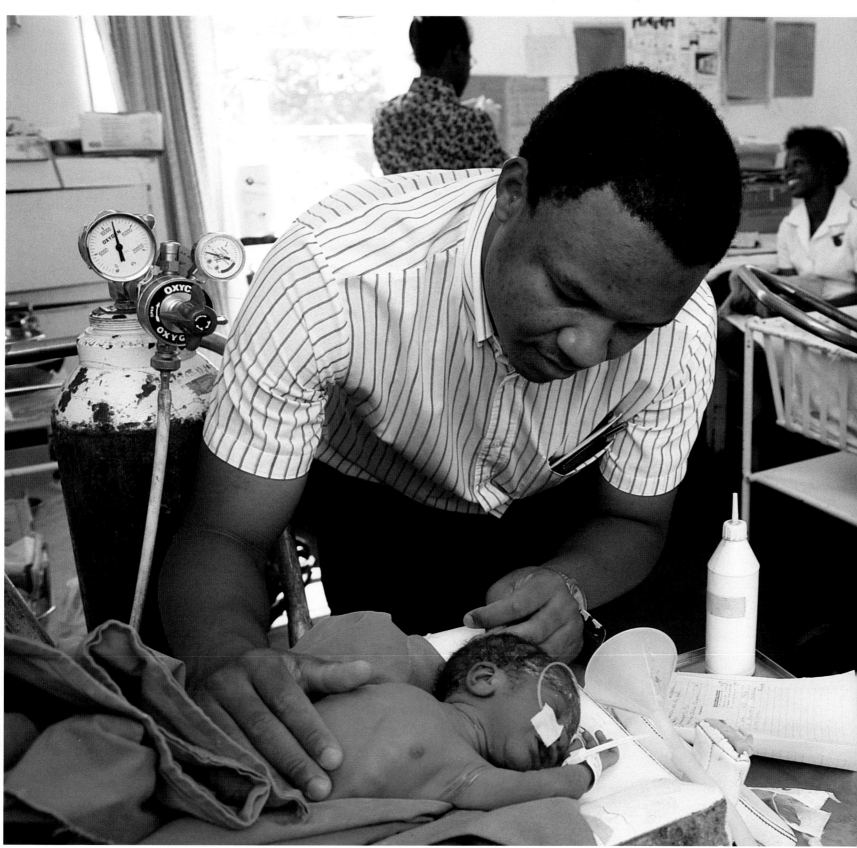

During the annual Independence Day celebrations, mass displays are performed by at least five thousand school children who are taught to use letters and boards that together portray various facets of the country's achievements.

The National Stadium has been the venue for the Independence Day celebrations every year since 1987. Apart from being one of the largest sporting venues in Africa, it is also extremely well equipped. Ultra-modern Swiss timing devices and two field cameras are linked to a control room, which co-ordinates displays on a television monitor several meters across. The starting blocks on the running tracks are fitted with electronic sensors to avoid false starts. The Stadium was designed by the Chinese Gansu Institute in 1983, and betrays the culture of its architects to the observant visitor; the numbering of the eight entrances on the perimeter runs counter-clockwise, contrary to that found in stadia throughout the rest of the world, which run clockwise.

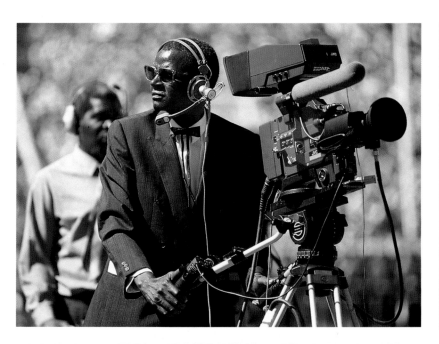

The working day in Zimbabwe starts early. At seven in the morning many urban streets are already crowded, and office workers are behind their desks by eight. The shortage of transport can mean waiting for a bus for hours. To get to work on time, many Zimbabweans have to leave for their work place long before sunrise, and they may not get home until well after the sun has set.

The fruit and vegetable markets (opposite) are alive well before any other part of the city. At four in the morning produce from the countryside is already filling the stalls.

A fantastic variety of fruits, seasonal vegetables and hand-dyed textiles is on sale in every urban market, such as these in Mbare and Gutu.

Despite modern healthcare facilities, traditional medicine still plays a major role in Zimbabwean life. In the markets, herbs and lotions are available for anything from simple headaches to chronic psychological problems. Aphrodisiacs are a persistent best seller.

Zimbabwe is alive with music. Bars, hotels, night clubs and city streets are sources of every conceivable musical offering.

Zimbabwe's most celebrated musician is Thomas Mapfumo (opposite). Before Independence, Mapfumo was jailed for his protest songs and general appeal to 'subversive' elements. Even today he still assumes the role of social commentator, and is one of several Zimbabwean artists to have established an international reputation.

Sport is a national obsession in Zimbabwe, both the climate and the space available making participation much easier than in Europe.

Until Independence, bowls had the highest number of participants, but it was superseded by soccer in the early 1980s. Now regarded as the country's national sport, football is able to pull in crowds 60,000 strong for big matches. Golf is another sport with a huge following, several players having made a deep impression on the international scene. Every town has at least one course, and there are over a dozen in the Harare district alone. The green pictured (below left) is set in the Vumba mountains, one of the most picturesque locations in the country.

Rugby is played to a particularly high standard at schools level; several school teams go on a foreign tour every year. Polo is a minority sport, but Zimbabwe fields a team of distinction which has played against most of the world's leading nations over the years.

In Bulawayo, streets are even wider than those of the capital, orginally designed so that a team of oxen could turn full circle. Three generations separate the construction of the new Municipal Offices designed by Harvey Buff and Partners in 1975 (below) from the Douslin building (right) built in 1902.

The copper-domed High Court was completed in 1938. Designed by Major William Roberts, it is typical of many public buildings built before the Second World War. There are other examples of this Italianate style elsewhere in the country, but few can match the High Court for sheer grandeur.

Behind the old colonial facades many of the shops still have a curiously dated air about them.

Architecture in Zimbabwe's other main towns reveals influences from many different cultures; (left) *a bar in Macheke, a church in Mutare and a hotel in Esigodini.*

Zimbabwe has few monuments to the Moslem faith, but the mosque in Kwe Kwe is one of the most prominent.

The Stock Exchange in Gweru was completed before the turn of the century (below left) *and is the oldest major building in the town. It was constructed during the surge of commercial activity which swept the country immediately after the First Chimurenga, and is a classic piece of colonial design, as is (below) the Magistrates' Court.*

THE INDUSTRIAL CORNUCOPIA

Unlike many African countries, Zimbabwe enjoys an abundance of raw materials for the development of its economy. The climate and soils allow agriculture to flourish, and the nation's mineral wealth must be the envy of many neighbouring states to the north. Nigeria has boomed and slumped because of its dependence on oil, Zambia has done the same with copper and other African countries have relied almost exclusively on cocoa, tea or tourism, but there is no one commodity on which Zimbabwe must depend. Instead, a host of different minerals and gemstones are all found in abundance within the country's borders. At the same time, the Zambezi presents a future source of ample hydro-electric power, while the wide range of agricultural produce is able to feed raw materials like wood, cotton, foodstuffs and tobacco into the industrial sector.

There is another reason why Zimbabwe is a good deal more self-reliant than her neighbours. During the UDI years, economic sanctions created a strong imperative to depend as little on the outside world as possible. Between 1965 and 1980 the two policies of import substitution and strict import control meant that the new state of Zimbabwe was to inherit a much more complete industrial infrastructure than would otherwise have been the case.

There is a downside to this, however. While self-reliance was encouraged during UDI, a degree of technological inertia was also created by the absence of contact with foreign industrial developments. Even today, much of the plant with which Zimbabwe's industries are operating dates back to the 1960s and before, effectively forcing the economy to function with one hand tied behind its back. The perennial shortage of foreign exchange has now put many industries in a Catch-22 situation. In order to buy new machinery the economy needs more hard currency, but in order to earn hard currency, Zimbabwe has to compete with countries which have much more modern machinery.

Despite the ambiguous legacy of UDI, Zimbabwe is responsible for more than 8,000 different products, ranging from agricultural vehicles to clothing and footwear, a level of diversity which puts the country head and shoulders above most of its neighbours.

Mining has taken place in the area for thousands of years. Excavations have uncovered a variety of ancient smelting techniques which were by no means restricted to iron. At least one Iron Age burial site on the banks of the Zambezi reveals much evidence of a thriving gold industry, for intricate necklaces of twisted gold as well as seashells set in gold have been unearthed there. The mining techniques were far from primitive; not only were timbers used, but good ventilation and lighting methods were employed as well.

The first Europeans to arrive in the area were drawn by wildly exaggerated accounts of the sheer quantity of gold which was waiting to be picked up. Inevitably they were disappointed; most of the gold reefs were too small and patchy for large scale exploitation, and the very elusiveness of the outcrops required a large initial investment, quite beyond the means of most prospectors.

Drilling the rock face to place charges hundreds of metres underground at a gold mine in Penhalonga.

Ironically, it was one such prospector who, almost by accident, was to make a discovery just as significant to the nation's economy as the mining of gold. Albert Giese, a young German, took a job in 1893 as a gold amalgamator at a mine in Tati in the west of the country. The following year he went on a hunting trip, heading in the general direction of the Victoria Falls. There, he was told by a local guide of "stones that burn" which could be found in a certain area. Hostile Ndebele warriors prevented his exploring further, but he returned the following year and found coal.

The Mashonaland Agency bought Giese's claims and engaged him to peg 1,000 square kilometres of territory, and after two years of prospecting and surveying the first five shafts were sunk. The Wankie (Rhodesia) Coal, Railway and Exploration Company was registered in 1898, this title being corrupted from Zvanki, the name of a chief who once ruled in the area. Initially, coal was transported from the colliery by ox-wagons before the 340 kilometre railway track from Bulawayo was completed in 1904. The railways, which had been using Welsh coal, became one of the colliery's early customers, while the surplus was exported to Kimberley in South Africa.

Each decade since the war has seen the arrival of another mineral in Zimbabwe's mining portfolio. In the 1950s, emeralds were discovered. The 1960s saw the beginning of nickel production on a grand scale. Platinum arrived in the 1970s, with the discovery that the Great Dyke might contain 4,000 million tonnes of reserves. By now, gold was recovering after a tempestuous two decades when interest had waxed and waned precariously. In 1973 alone, over fifty new mines were opened, bringing the total number in the country to 530.

With Independence in 1980, Mugabe's policy of conciliation was met with relief by the chiefs in the mining industry. There was an initial period of instability caused in part by the violent activities of Ndebele dissidents, but by the mid 1980s the situation began to improve. As the country became more stable politically, departments of mining and engineering were opened at the University of Zimbabwe. The teething troubles of the new order appear to be over and growth is the order of the day, although the endless shortage of foreign exchange is making investment in competitive new plant very difficult.

Today, gold is easily Zimbabwe's most valuable mineral, coming from over four hundred mines around the country. Gold alone earns over a third of all Zimbabwe's mining revenue. Nickel and asbestos make up another third, while the remainder is accounted for by coal, copper, chromite, iron ore, tin, silver, graphite and a dozen other minerals.

Both mining and agriculture supply raw materials to the manufacturing sector of the economy, which contributes the largest share of the country's economic output. Zimbabwe's railway network has been the principal factor in determining the location of factories. Until the Federal era, Bulawayo was the main industrial centre because it was on the railway line from South Africa, and because there was easy access to the Hwange coalfields. When Salisbury (Harare) was chosen as the Federal capital, many factories were established there, and the city became the largest single market in the Federation, a dominance which has continued to this day. Together, Harare and Bulawayo account for two thirds of Zimbabwe's industrial output. In the east, Mutare is also important because it lies on the rail route to the port of Beira in Mozambique, and because it is close to the country's main timber growing area.

The biggest metal manufacturing plant in the country is to be found in the Midlands. The Zimbabwe Iron and Steel Corporation (ZISCO) is one of the biggest single employers in the nation, with a labour force of over six thousand. At Redcliffe, ZISCO runs two enormous blast furnaces, and with its ancillary plant, the Corporation is capable of producing almost a million tons each year of non-flat metal products such as blooms, billets, ploughshares, bars and rods, pig iron and steel wire. ZISCO has spawned many enterprises based on steel and metal fabrication. Heavy engineering firms design and produce machinery, equipment and spares for other industries, while other concerns have built a solid reputation for the original design of metal tools, particularly agricultural implements suitable for local conditions.

While the mining industry supplies metal manufacturing companies, other concerns are able to tap into the agricultural sector. In the textile industry, for example, David Whitehead is the biggest consumer of Zimbabwe's home-grown cotton lint. Like ZISCO, its plants at Kadoma and Chegutu employ thousands, and cotton products are Zimbabwe's most important foreign exchange earner after tobacco. However, the shortage of foreign exchange, together with economies of scale in Europe and cheaper labour costs in the Far East, make it hard for Zimbabwean textile manufacturers to remain competitive in the international arena. It is an achievement that in such shops as Marks and Spencer in Britain the words 'Made in Zimbabwe' can be found on some of their clothes.

Agriculture also supplies the foodstuffs industry, which comprises meat slaughtering and processing, fruit and vegetable canning and preservation, grain mill products and animal feeds. The increase in real incomes since Independence has led to a growing demand for alcoholic beverages. Most of Zimbabwe's alcohol requirements are met by the sugar mill distillery in the south-eastern lowveld. Wine is produced locally and exported, as is larger, to several neighbouring countries as well as Europe. Soft drinks and carbonated waters are consumed by locals, but export potential is limited by the high bulk/low value characteristics of these products, and the fact that neighbouring countries have their own plants.

There is another sector of the Zimbabwean economy, quite removed from the large manufacturing concerns, which is worthy of mention. The so-called 'informal sector' also makes a substantial contribution to the economy of Zimbabwe. The term refers to small-scale income generating activities which do not abide by formal contractual rules or regulations. Thus, many activities in Zimbabwe, be they carpentry, upholstering, tin-smithing, welding, brick making or motor-repair are frequently unlicensed, and it is difficult to measure the true value of their input into the economy. The rapid population increase in Zimbabwe, together with the influx of rural immigrants to the cities, has given rise to a large number of men and women earning their living in this way. Traditionally, the sector was occupied by people with little schooling, but with the sharp increase in access to secondary education since Independence, a number of workers now have a solid academic background, a visible symptom of the formal sector's difficulty in absorbing all of the country's school leavers.

The Zimbabwe Iron and Steel Company (ZISCO)
is one of the country's most important manufacturers.
ZISCO is capable of producing 800,000 tonnes
a year of non-flat steel products, such as blooms,
billets, ploughshares, angles, and specialised
industrial components.

Its customers include the makers of agricultural
implements, builders of lorries, railway rolling stock
and tracks, nut and bolt manufacturers and
construction companies.

ZISCO is one of Zimbabwe's biggest employers,
with some 6,000 people engaged in its operation.
When their families are taken into consideration, it is
estimated that some 50,000 Zimbabweans depend
directly on the company for their economic well-being.

FOLLOWING PAGE: *Steel is poured into a mould for the creation of a locomotive component at a railway maintenance shed in Bulawayo.*

To sustain one of the finest
transport networks in Africa,
Zimbabwe has developed a high
degree of self-reliance. The
railway maintenance sheds at
Bulawayo are constantly
(and successfully) engaged in
prolonging the life of the
country's locomotives - much to
the delight of railway buffs from
all over the world.

Fitters service a jet aircraft engine. The Ministry of Transport's team of experienced engineers is constantly strengthened by the arrival of bright young graduates from the University.

Air Zimbabwe's First Officer Emily Njovani is one of many African women now breaking traditional professional barriers in Zimbabwe.

THE ANIMAL KINGDOM

Few visitors to Zimbabwe travel around the country without wanting to savour its fabulous wildlife heritage. Unlike some other tourist destinations on the continent – notably Kenya and South Africa – hundreds of species of animal and bird life can still be seen in an environment not far removed from that of pre-colonial Africa. Moreover, this is likely to be the case for several future generations at least, thanks to one of the most enlightened policies of wildlife conservation and management in the world. While some factions would allow the unbridled depletion of countless species, and others – often obsessive 'liberals' from the affluent west – have condemned any hunting as heresy, Zimbabwe has steered a pragmatic middle path. Safari hunting has become a controlled and profitable way of using wildlife as a renewable natural resource. This involves a relatively small kill-rate, which brings in far more revenue per animal than would be possible when cropping for meat.

Quotas for trophy animals in each safari area and Communal Land concession are set by the Department of National Parks and Wildlife Management. They are calculated on the basis of aerial censuses and ground reconnaissance by their staff, as well as reports from professional hunters. This philosophy is immediately evident to anyone walking the streets of central Harare: there can be few countries in the world which have such a variety of ivory goods on sale – in particular exquisitely carved tusks in the form of miniature friezes – and for such a market to be entirely legal. The government's argument is simple: Zimbabwe already has a viable population of elephants, and an excess would damage the environment. It therefore makes sense for controlled culling to take place.

Hunting is now developing fastest on commercial farmland. Today, many extensive cattle ranches have either incorporated wildlife or abandoned cattle altogether in favour of wildlife systems which depend on safari operations for their profits. This is not only a sound move economically but it also makes ecological sense. In areas of low rainfall and poor soils – about two-thirds of the country – the overgrazing of domestic animals has made soil erosion a very serious problem. The incorporation of non-carnivorous wildlife varies the burden on the land while diversifying the farmer's source of income.

Another factor with a crucial effect on the country's resources is the very success of the tourist industry. It is not simply wildlife in Zimbabwe that visitors come to see. The many lakes, mountains, rivers and above all the Victoria Falls, are natural assets which need to be protected indefinitely if Zimbabwe is to retain its unique characteristics. Tourism is one of the country's most important growth industries: the infrastructure of hotels and communications is excellent, but the increasing instability of other African destinations is bringing more holiday makers to Zimbabwe than ever before.

But the Ministry of Tourism is not flinging the doors wide open to everyone. By deliberately concentrating on higher cost quality facilities, Zimbabwe is aiming to earn the maximum revenue while suffering minimal environmental damage from its tourist industry. Zimbabwe's tourist venues are thus spared the profusion of fast food joints, coach parks and cheap souvenir shops which adorn the most famous sites in Egypt, Morocco and Kenya. Another important development has been the encouragement of local Zimbabweans to enjoy their own heritage, thus heightening their awareness of the assets which the country has to offer.

Astonishingly, the giraffe has just seven vertebrae in its neck, just like any other mammal. In order to protect the brain from the weight of blood rushing to its head when it is drinking, it has an intricate circulatory system which relieves the pressure.

Kudu (below) are among the most elegant of antelopes, with their spiral horns and dignified air. They are particularly easy to find, since they come to the watering holes in the open in the middle of the day. Female kudu are a favourite prey of wild dogs.

The photographs taken on these and the following ten pages are mostly taken in Hwange National Park, the largest piece of land in the country which has been set aside for the specific purpose of wildlife conservation.

During the dry months, buffalo herds two to three thousand strong often make their way across the open plains. Although they are an important prey species for lions, they don't give in without a fight; many is the occasion when a large group of them have successfully beaten off a lion attack, giving commercial hunters good reason to treat them with respect. At night, however, they are much more vulnerable.

Wildebeest are not indigenous to the Park but immigrated from Botswana during the 1930s. Even today they are confined to the grassy plains in the south.

Cheetah are a rare sight, but are being found more and more on nearby farms. This is because farmers in the region have started to diversify their activities, taking tourists onto their land for photographic safaris. Since impala who stray onto farmland are no longer shot so readily, cheetah frequently come in search for them.

Gemsbok are rare visitors to Hwange and are usually found on the Kalahari sands close to the Botswana border.

Zebra stallions wrestle with one another like playful schoolboys. In fact the tussling has a serious intent - more often than not, the males are competing with one another for the favour of a mate.

To human eyes, the stripes of a zebra make it conspicuous, but they are a highly effective camouflage in the bush against predators who can only see in monochrome. No two zebras' stripes are alike: as with human fingerprints, each pattern is unique to its wearer.

The birdlife in Zimbabwe is prolific, and is becoming the focus of many ornithologists. More than six hundred species of bird life have been found within the country's borders. The white-fronted bee-eater (above) *can often be seen on sticks without leaves. Some observers theorise that the bright colours of these birds have evolved to convince insects that they are flowers, thereby attracting them for the purpose of pollination. A different fate awaits them.*

The ostrich (opposite) *is the largest bird in the world. Despite the fact that it has lost its ability to fly, it can run at surprising speeds. In South Africa, they are even used for racing, and are strong enough to be ridden by a jockey.*

FOLLOWING PAGE: *The fish eagle,* (top left) *has suffered more than most from the continued use of DDT; the shells of its eggs are measurably weakened by the chemical, which has been banned in the rest of the world.*

The other species are (middle left) *the black-winged stilt,* (bottom left) *the kori bustard,* (top right) *the goliath heron,* (bottom right) *the white egret and* (facing page) *the saddle-billed stork.*

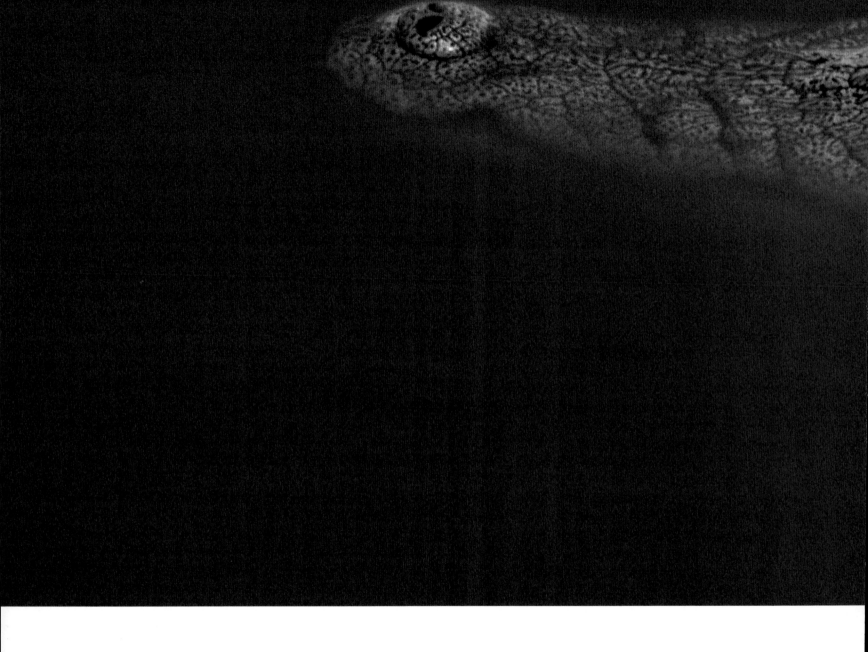

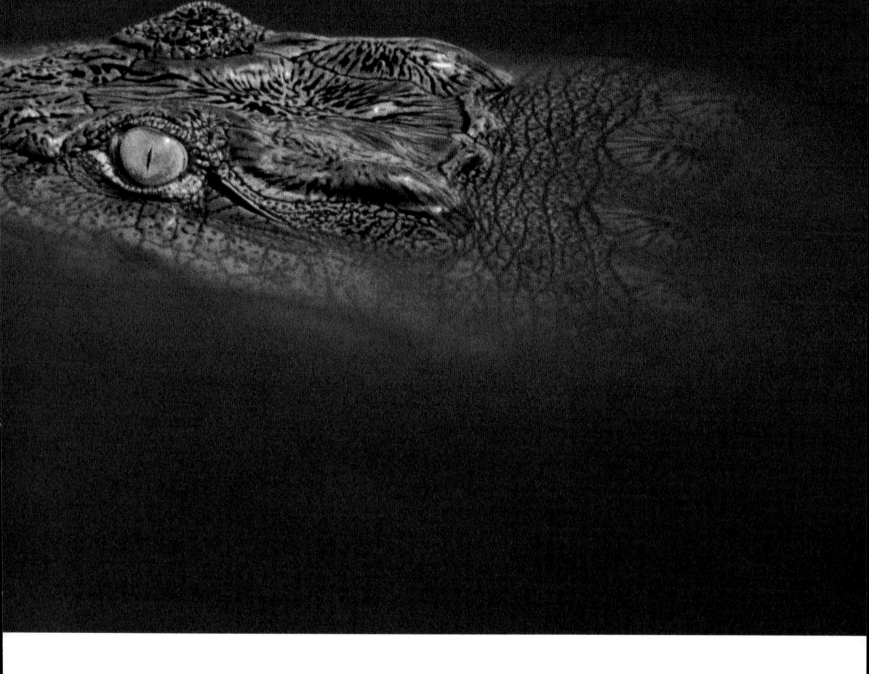

Crocodiles are living fossils. Their direct ancestors were roaming the earth 300 million years ago, 100 million years before the great dinosaurs evolved. As if to demonstrate this, crocodiles still exude a primeval air, adult males reaching over four metres in length on occasion. As reptiles, their metabolism is affected by extremes of hot and cold; consequently they spend much of their time regulating their body temperature by basking in the sun or cooling off in water.

Kudu (above); *Impala*
(right). *During the rainy season
game is more difficult to spot
because of the thickness of the
foliage. The best time to view
animals is during the dry months
from May to October, when they
come out of the bush to drink
at the waterholes.*

In Hwange, nearly every water hole has its resident family of baboons. Loyalties within a troop run deep; individuals are quick to protect one another when there is any sign of danger, and a mother bereaved of her child will carry its body around with her for days, obviously in mourning. The mother (above) protectively holds on to her child's tail, and after a cold winter's night in mid July (right and below) the youngsters play hard to warm themselves up.

THE WEALTH OF THE LAND

Agriculture is Zimbabwe's lifeblood. Not only does it feed the nation, it provides a surplus of food for export, as well as a wide array of raw materials for the manufacturing sector. The country's range of activities is marvellously diverse. Maize is the principal food crop, but there is no shortage of sorghum, millet, wheat, barley, oats, soybeans, groundnuts, sunflowers, vegetables and fruit. The main cash crops are tobacco - far and away the most important - cotton, sugar, tea and coffee. Horticulture is a new and burgeoning industry, and is set to become a major export earner. There is also abundant livestock activity, consisting mainly in the rearing of cattle, pigs, sheep, goats and poultry. Farm-reared wildlife is also being explored. In all, agriculture employs a quarter of Zimbabwe's working population, and generates over a third of the country's foreign exchange earnings.

Not surprisingly, Zimbabwe's farming infrastructure has been determined largely by its political history, for the dispute over land was a central issue during the colonial period. At the end of the nineteenth century, the principal attraction for many of the first white settlers was gold. Once it became clear that claims over the country's gold wealth had been exaggerated, there was a surge in interest in cattle ranching and farming land. The British South Africa Company made this cheaply and easily available to whites, regardless of who was living on it at the time. After the wars of the 1890s, political and military power was vested entirely in the settlers, and there was little to prevent them from helping themselves to the best land in the country.

By the 1920s, the loose policy of setting aside reserves for Africans became more clearly focused, culminating in the Land Apportionment Act of 1930. This allocated fixed reserves, generally poor, remote and inadequate, to the local people. Where necessary they were resettled there, while their former lands became 'European Areas'. Special 'Purchase Areas' became available to African commercial farmers (as distinct from peasant farmers), which could be bought and developed in the same way as the land allocated to Europeans.

The pattern thus created sustained itself until the eve of Independence, and even now is the subject of much debate in the political arena. Essentially, there are four distinct types of farming area:

- The larger commercial farms which had been exclusively in the hands of white farmers, and comprise over a third of Zimbabwe's total land area. There are still over four thousand farms in this sector, and they generate most of the country's market surplus. Their success is due to the quality of the soil and the capital facilities which have been available to make the best use of it, as well as the expertise of the farmers themselves.

- The smaller commercial farms, which used to be the African Purchase Lands, and occupy only four per cent of the country's land area.

On the Vumba Estates, in spite of the machinery available, manpower is often more suitable. The huge areas of forest need careful supervision during the dry season because of the risk of fire.

- The Communal Lands, formerly known as the Tribal Trust Lands, which occupy 42 per cent of the country, and are home to nine million people, well over half of Zimbabwe's population. Most of the farmers on these lands are engaged in some form of subsistence activity, but overpopulation and limited resources have resulted in deterioration of the land.

- Some Resettlement Areas which have been established since Independence as part of the Government's land redistribution efforts. The Government buys commercial farming land and makes it available to farmers from those Communal Lands which are under pressure from people and their livestock.

Of all the country's activities, agriculture has undergone the most striking changes since Independence. The most important development has been the entry of many peasant farmers into the cash economy as a direct result of access to extended credit facilities, which have given them the chance to buy fertiliser and equipment. This is borne out most visibly in the dramatic increase in production of the country's principal food crop, maize, from the Communal Lands. In 1979, only 4.8 per cent of the country's maize production came from this sector. Now, that figure is well over 60 per cent. While this trend will to some extent mean an improvement in living standards among rural farmers, there is a very real danger that it might be offset in the long term by the effects of soil erosion, which is acute in many of the country's poorest farming districts. In some areas, soil is being lost at a rate of more than forty tonnes per hectare per year.

In purely economic terms, Zimbabwe's most important single crop is tobacco. Despite campaigns against smoking in Europe and elsewhere, the demand for cigarettes worldwide is increasing, and Zimbabwe is one of the chief beneficiaries - so long as the price of tobacco stays high. In a good year, tobacco can account for a fifth of the country's foreign exchange earnings. Furthermore, tobacco provides a livelihood, directly or indirectly, for over half a million Zimbabweans. Although it is an exacting crop to grow, and there are those who cast aspersions on the morality of producing it, the economic benefits which tobacco brings to the country are so overwhelming that there is no credible substitute in the foreseeable future.

As far as livestock is concerned, Zimbabwe is first and foremost beef country. The nation's beef is among the finest in the world, and it has become so popular in Europe that the scale of current exports makes it impossible to satisfy the home market, which is rapidly expanding. Once again, the preoccupation which cattle is largely a product of the country's colonial history. It is a curious paradox that African countries have a wide variety of large mammal fauna, and yet their livestock farmers betray an almost obsessive interest in cattle. This is largely because settlers brought in the animals which they best knew how to rear, and they were at the same time unaware of the potential offered by indigenous wild animals. This situation is has been accentuated by the fact that game is traditionally associated with sport and leisure in the minds of many Europeans, and few had the insight to husband any other livestock than cattle. It remains to be seen how sustainable beef exporting in such large quantities will be in the long term. Low rainfall and poor soils in many beef livestock areas mean that the carrying capacity in much of the country will always be severely limited.

Outside the commercial farms, the relationship between men and their cattle is a very different one. Far fewer cattle in the Communal Lands are slaughtered for beef, and this is due in part to the esteem in which cattle are traditionally held.

One of the most exciting developments in recent years has been the success of horticulture, a direct result of the economic sanctions imposed on the country following UDI in 1965. Until that time horticulture played a very minor role in the country's economy. But the sudden scarcity of foreign currency and high prices of imports gave it a boost, and production began in earnest in the east, with fruit and vegetables being transported daily to markets in Harare and Bulawayo. The wide variety of climate and soils within Zimbabwe's borders makes it possible to produce over sixty types of fruit and vegetables, as well as grapes for wine.

More recent still has been the surge in flower production. An enormous potential has now been discovered for the export of flowers to Europe during the northern hemisphere's winter months, and flower sales abroad are likely to become a valuable earner of foreign exchange. At the height of the export season some three hundred tonnes of flowers are air-freighted out of Zimbabwe every week.

Two major issues have preoccupied farmers in recent years. One was the drought of 1992, which led to the deaths of thousands of head of cattle and other livestock, not to mention acute human suffering in many rural areas. The country's economic growth rate fell to minus 6 per cent, and over US $700 million worth of grain had to be imported for emergency food relief. The farming community bounced back when good rains came the following year, but the effect on the economy of the drought will be long lasting.

The second is the prospect of massive land redistribution. The government's stated plans to purchase 5 million hectares worries Zimbabwe's 4,300 large scale farmers, nearly all of them white. They may have seized their land from the Africans during the colonial era, but they produce important export commodities and domestic food crops. Economists, however, warn that no matter what colour the farmers are, they must maintain and even improve their productivity if Zimbabwe is to prosper in the next century.

Forestry dates from the 1920s when the construction of railways created a demand for wooden sleepers. Pit props were also needed to satisfy the burgeoning mining industry.

The country's indigenous trees were essentially hardwood, but once it was realised that this alone was not adequate to sustain a viable forestry industry, softwood plantations were established in the east of the country, where the higher rainfall and altitude enabled them to flourish.

Today, 95% of the forestry industry is reliant on softwoods such as pine and eucalyptus, which are used for packaging, tobacco casing, fruit boxes, telephone poles and pulp. Hardwoods are used for furniture, paqué floors and doors. The Forestry Commission and firms in the private sector are vigorously seeking to add value to their produce by exporting furniture components rather than unprocessed timber.

Despite extensive planting in the Communal Areas the intense demand for firewood has led, in the words of one civil servant, to much 'de facto resource sharing' - a delicious euphemism for theft.

In some areas, notably the Save River Valley, virtually all tree cover has now been removed. The Forestry Commission broadcasts four radio programmes a month, two in Shona and two in Ndebele, to heighten awareness of the role which tree planting and fire protection play in the future of the country's environment. The Commission is also a research institute, investigating the production of different species.

The climate in the Eastern Highlands is ideal for the optimum growth of eucalyptus (above, below) and pine. The world's tallest eucalyptus trees are found not in Australia, their original home, but here in Zimbabwe. At the same time, pine trees grow roughly twice as fast here as they do in Scandinavia. Although commercially successful, pine trees are not indigenous to Africa, and local fauna have not adapted to them. A walk through one of the plantations is almost an other-worldly experience, so devoid are the trees of birds and animals. In contrast, the few remaining hardwood forests still thrive on the interdependence of plant, insect and animal life.

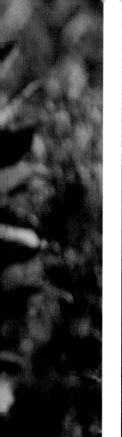

Tobacco plays a vital role in Zimbabwe's export economy. Despite sustained anti-smoking campaigns in Europe and the United States, the demand for cigarettes worldwide is increasing, and this crop is likely to remain of supreme importance for the foreseeable future. Zimbabwe produces some of the highest quality tobacco in the world, most of which is exported to the European Community.

Tobacco plants need a lot of moisture, and thus seedlings are planted at the beginning of the rains in November. The most suitable soils are light and well drained because tobacco is sensitive to water-logging.

The main auction floor at Harare (left). At the beginning of each day's sale, trolleys holding a bale each are lined up and opened so that prospective buyers can feel and smell the produce. Once the bale has gone to the highest bidder it is labelled with the name of the buying company and packed for export.

The Aberfoyle tea estates (opposite) *cover the slopes at the northern end of the Honde Valley near the border with Mozambique. Tea production began in the 1950s and underwent rapid expansion, so the entire country is now self-sufficient.*

For tea of the highest quality, (below) *only the tips of the bushes are ever picked.*

Hops are one of the newest crops in Zimbabwe, being first grown successfully in 1986. Indigenous to temperate latitudes, they require long hours of daylight during the summer months. Since Zimbabwe is never exposed to more than fourteen hours of continuous sunshine, artificial lighting is needed to create suitable conditions. In the dark of an African evening, hop plantations make a bizarre sight to passing motorists. The production of bottled lager beer is rapidly expanding, and it is now being exported to Europe and the United States.

Sunflowers are a useful cash crop whose seeds are processed to supplement the country's supply of corn oil. They are particularly attractive to communal farmers because they are cheap to cultivate and provide a reasonable return. Commercial farmers are now taking an increasing interest in growing sunflowers in the marginal areas.

White commercial farmers still play an immensely important role in the country's economy. Many members of the white community left after Independence, but thousands more took a conscious decision to stay on. The concept of a white African may be hard for some to grasp, but Zimbabwe is a much-loved homeland for many of these people. To most white Zimbabweans, the rest of the world is a foreign place.

ndnuts are another favourite for communal farmers, a ready source of protein and remarkably drought nt. Great potential exists for the export of confec- ry peanuts worldwide. Mangetouts are exported to pe during the Northern Hemisphere's winter months.

Until recently flowers were regarded principally as an export crop, earning foreign exchange from the markets of Europe when their own flowers were out of season. However, the European tradition of giving flowers as a gift has begun to catch on at home. February 14th, 1991 was a historic day for Zimbabwe; for the first time, the local supply of flowers was unable to meet the demand on Valentine's Day.

Most coffee is produced on commercial plantations, but communal farmers are now beginning to grow the crop in the Honde and Rusitu valleys. Coffee is a major export industry, but although a valuable earner of foreign exchange, it is difficult to grow well, requiring careful nurturing at every stage of production.

The seedlings need regular watering and the beans have to be picked manually because they are graded at the same time. Even when drying they are turned by hand. Consequently the industry is very labour intensive, employing some 30,000 people.

Most of the country's plantations are in the Eastern Highlands. The mountains behind the Charleswood Estate (above) belong to the Chimanimani range.

The commercial production of grapes (above) began during the UDI years when wine was difficult to import, and is now a well established industry.

Zimbabwean cotton (right) is hand-picked, and hence of extremely high quality.

The Mazoe Citrus Estates were established at the turn of the century, and their produce is celebrated throughout southern Africa. The quality of Mazoe orange juice is so revered that homesick Zimbabweans stationed abroad often receive it as a gift from visiting friends and relatives.

FOLLOWING PAGE: Young stock and steers at an early morning round-up. Cattle play a very important part in Zimbabwe's agriculture, since much of the country is not suitable for crop production. The commercial cattle ranches in the dry south of the country can be many thousands of hectares in size.

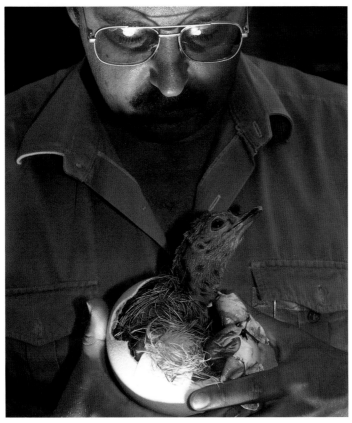

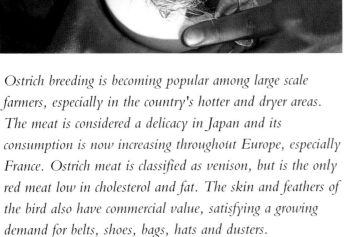

Ostrich breeding is becoming popular among large scale farmers, especially in the country's hotter and dryer areas. The meat is considered a delicacy in Japan and its consumption is now increasing throughout Europe, especially France. Ostrich meat is classified as venison, but is the only red meat low in cholesterol and fat. The skin and feathers of the bird also have commercial value, satisfying a growing demand for belts, shoes, bags, hats and dusters.

FOLLOWING PAGE: Commercial farmers are diversifying into game ranching because it offers high returns and is a useful supplement to beef.

Zimbabwe has the largest rhino concentration left in Africa, but with incursions by armed gangs who use paramilitary tactics, the problem of poaching is not easily solved. Despite the translocation of rhinos to private farms and wildlife estates, poachers have not been deterred. Rhino continue to be killed on a daily basis, and the population is still declining. The commercial cultivation of rhino horn is now being entertained by some farmers.

THE PASTORAL DREAM

It would be very easy to believe that the countryside in Zimbabwe is sparsely populated. Anyone driving a car on the long, straight road from Harare to the Eastern Highlands, for example, could be forgiven for thinking that the surrounding plains are almost completely devoid of people. In fact, nothing could be further from the truth. Before Independence the principal transport arteries were designed to join the main trading centres and to service the larger commercial farms. The thousands of small villages where Africans lived were simply bypassed, giving an impression from the roadside that there are few people to be found between the towns. In reality, no fewer than seven out of every ten Zimbabweans live in the countryside, and their principal means of transport is walking.

Equally erroneous would be the idea that life in rural Zimbabwe has remained unchanged for centuries. This line may read well in tourist brochures, but it is again quite false. As long as man has dwelt in this land, his social system and way of life have been constantly evolving. In particular, the arrival of Europeans in the 1890s brought the cash economy and urban culture, placing the old order under ever-increasing pressure for change. More recently, the population explosion and the fight for Independence have further forced the pace. The small cluster of grass-roofed huts which symbolises both home and community to millions of Zimbabweans may represent a long-lost dream to many Europeans, but at the end of the twentieth century it is slowly dissolving.

In pre-colonial times, the traditional village, consisting of the headman, his family and others linked to him by kinship or other social bonds was once a place where the warmth of domestic life extended into the community. The headman was looked upon as the father of all who lived under him, and outsiders who joined the little society were as much a part of it as the headman's own family. They became permanent members from the moment they were allocated land to cultivate, and could not thereafter be ejected. All land among the Shona belonged to the chief, whose right to it was believed to have been granted by the great god, Mwari. In this capacity the chief distributed the land among his people and collected tribute from them.

Under European rule, everything changed. Ultimate sovereignty was shifted to the Government, and chiefs could only allocate land which was apportioned to them by the new authorities. In addition, the large number of migrant workers away from home at any one time led to divided loyalties between traditional and political leaders. Urban townships, business centres and enterprises in other areas fell outside the chiefs' jurisdiction. Throughout the twentieth century, the chiefly role consistently lost ground to the new social forces at play. Finally, during the Liberation War, the Rhodesian authorities brought many people from their scattered homes to live in 'protected villages', partly to shelter those who did not want to co-operate with the insurgents, and partly to restrict those who did. Such villages are of course long gone, but the effect of this policy has been lasting.

Apart from political and military forces, religion has also deeply influenced rural life. From the middle of the nineteenth century the Anglican, Catholic, Methodist, and Dutch Reformed Churches, as well as several others, all began to use schools as a means of instilling their values into African youths. At first the suspicion of African elders towards the missions prevented the attendance of most children, but when it became known that those who could read and write were able to earn better wages in employment, this reluctance began to evaporate. Rural missions have also provided extensive medical services, agricultural training and other economic advice. As with other African countries, the most prominent members of Zimbabwean society have often been deeply influenced by missionaries in their childhood.

But the unsung heroes of the Zimbabwean countryside are undoubtedly the women. Those who live on the Communal Lands work particularly hard for little return. Agriculture is far and away their most important activity, especially in those areas where the men are migrant labourers in town. With their husbands away from home for long periods, many women are *de facto* head of the household.

Women in the countryside will often start their working day at four thirty in the morning and finish at nine at night. Apart from house cleaning and looking after the children, they have to take maize to mills for grinding, often carrying fifteen kilos for hours there and back. They also cover large distances on foot to do all the necessary shopping and collect firewood. Back home, they have to grind by hand cereal crops other than maize, as well as groundnuts to make peanut butter. Their time can also be taken up keeping chickens, weeding vegetable plots and selling cash crops.

All of these tasks become intensified during funerals and weddings, and if their menfolk are away working on commercial farms or in a city, women may also find themselves herding cattle through the summer months, taking them to dips once a week, and guarding the vegetable plots against baboons.

Ironically, the increased educational opportunities for children have had the effect of increasing yet further the workload of mothers who had formerly relied on their children for help in the daily routine. Rural families are normally expected to contribute to their offspring's education by providing labour for tasks like the making of bricks for school buildings. Once again, this is usually a woman's work.

Although Zimbabwean society carries a tradition of male domination, the Government is committed to the emancipation of rural women. Much has been achieved since Independence to break the age-old constraints which have kept them subservient. Not only are more girls going to agricultural colleges, where they now make up 25 per cent of students, but women of all ages are very often forming co-operatives to increase their efficiency. As a result they are becoming very much more productive. Before Independence, communal farmers, most of whom were women, produced five per cent of the country's staple crop, maize. Now, that figure is 60 per cent.

Despite the many social and cultural obstacles, agriculture on the Communal Lands has proven remarkably resilient. Since Independence, considerable help has been offered to peasant farmers, and their productivity has been increased by piped water, hybrid grains and chemical fertilisers. These developments have come hand in hand with improved roads and marketing services. The infrastructure of the Communal Lands has also been improved, with special facilities and guaranteed prices for peasant farmers to encourage production. Above all, an ambitious resettlement programme designed to give peasant farmers access to the better land once only available to settlers is now under way.

But the slow pace of the land reform programme is frustrating for rural people. Soil erosion and drought have conspired to force many peasants onto the richer commercial farmland, much of which they claim is under-utilised. Classified as squatters, these peasants have often been forcibly evicted by the army and police. This has caused friction in many parts of the country, arousing demands for a faster implementation of the more equitable land distribution which was promised by the liberation movements before Independence.

Elsewhere on the agenda, there have been more striking achievements, particularly in the field of health. Hundreds of primary health care facilities have been constructed in rural areas, and the combination of preventive medicine and child immunisation has served to reduce infant mortality dramatically. The Ministry of Health has adopted the unusual policy of working alongside, rather than against, traditional healers. Members of ZINATHA, the Zimbabwe Traditional Healers' Association, do not as a rule resist western medicine, but seek to complement it with their own procedures for securing physical and spiritual health. It is not unknown for patients to be released from rural government hospitals so that they can be seen by a local *n'anga*, or healer. The only condition attached is that they must return by nightfall. However, *n'angas* are not allowed to practice on hospital grounds.

The general improvement in health, particularly among children, has led to a marked rise in population growth for Zimbabwe as a whole, putting pressure on many young people to seek employment in the cities. Only time will tell whether land reform will enable the rural children of the next century to secure a living where they are, or whether the pull of the bright lights will urbanise the country's population irreversibly.

These days, some women engaged in the informal sector are over-qualified for the work they do. This girl (top) from Midlands Province holds eight 'O'-levels and may well be going on to University.

The weaving of baskets (above) is just one traditional craft which fulfills the double function of generating income and consolidating a sense of community within this rural village near Lupane.

Since ancient times, rural dwellings in Zimbabwe have been built on the rock outcrops (opposite) which are scattered throughout the country, like these near Masvingo. This is not the safest place for them to be; every year, about three hundred people are killed by lightening which strikes the exposed huts.

FOLLOWING PAGE: The little girl in a village near Masvingo is carrying the fruit of a baobab tree, from which cream of tartar is obtained.

143

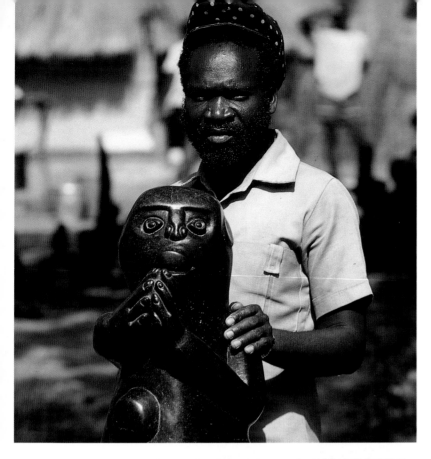

Modern sculpture from Zimbabwe enjoys a world-wide reputation. As a school of art its origins date back no further than the 1950s, but four decades have been enough for several exponents to become internationally recognised. The works of the late Joseph Ndandarika, Sylvester Mubayi, Henry Munyaradzi and several others can fetch large sums on the international art market, and there are many lesser figures aspiring to the same heights. Behind them there are thousands more whose works fill the street corners and curio shops, satisfying the demand from tourists for a cheap souvenir of the country.

The work is commonly described as 'Shona sculpture', but there are in fact two distinct schools. One represents the work of the Shona people, its greater naturalism affording easy access to westerners. The other is known as the Tengenenge, taking its name from the remarkable community of artists who spend their days carving serpentine on an old farm just south of the Zambezi escarpment. Its qualities are more robust and less compromising, owing less to the Shona culture than to the personalities of its polyglot exponents - Zambians, Malawians, Angolans and Mozambicans among them. Tengenenge was founded by Tom Blomefield, who took over the farm in the 1940s and turned to sculpture when his tobacco production business began to founder during the sanctions era. There are now over a hundred artists associated with the farm, many of whom are resident. Several of Zimbabwe's biggest names are products of this community, including Bernard Matamera (opposite page).

The main obstacle to recognition for aspiring sculptors is the sheer distance of Zimbabwe from the art markets of Europe and North America, and the consequent cost of transporting pieces that often weigh a hundred kilos or more.

147

During certain religious festivals, it is not uncommon to see thousands of people all dressed in white, praying on a patch of bare earth.

Familiarly known as the Vapostori, the followers of the Apostolic faith can be found all over the country. The most spectacular celebration of all marks the Passover, when tens of thousands will gather for a period of several days. The Vapostori constitute not one sect but many which have grown and diversified over the last three generations.

Some, (including the one seen on these pages) attract members from all walks of life, including university graduates, teachers, members of the army and police force, nurses, journalists and district administrators. Others have been known to shun employment in the formal sector, relying instead on cottage industries to survive.

The large gatherings in the open involve singing and worship, often lasting for days. People come from all over the country and abroad to attend the major festivals. Despite the modern accoutrements, they are reminiscent of the first Christian gatherings in the ancient land of Palestine. The locally made tape recorders held by the men on the previous page are recording a speech by Archbishop Paul Mwazha.

During the religious service the men and women sit apart and, as in many other religions, the women cover their heads. Since everything has to be carried to the meeting, the supper being prepared on the fires (below) tends to be simple.

Every year between September and January there takes place that most important of rituals, the rainmaking ceremony. The ceremony has roots in the distant past but is still performed today in many rural villages, such as this one in Chief Hwange's territory. When the rains are due, beer is brewed and everyone is summoned to a sacred place, usually on a nearby hill. Traditional dances are then performed, generating a hysteria which can be quite literally entrancing for the participants. The sweet, innocuous brew is consumed in large quantities.

The singing and dancing are seen as a way of appeasing the ancestral spirits; traditionally, the Shona believe that the spirits of their ancestors control the rain, sending storms when they are happy and drought to express their displeasure at some worldly event.

Shops in rural Zimbabwe
are more than just an
outlet for retail goods;
they double as important
meeting places, where cash
and gossip are exchanged
in equal measure.

Many rural areas
have been declared
'growth points' to
promote the policy of
decentralisation. By
investing in hitherto
neglected regions the
authorities hope to
convince the rural
population, especially
school leavers, to stay
where they are and
develop the local economy.

One of the most dramatic achievements since Independence has been the huge increase in maize production from some of the poorest farm areas. In 1979, farmers on the Communal Lands were responsible for just 4.8 per cent of the country's total output. Today that figure is well over 60 per cent. Extended credit facilities for fertiliser and equipment have been largely responsible.

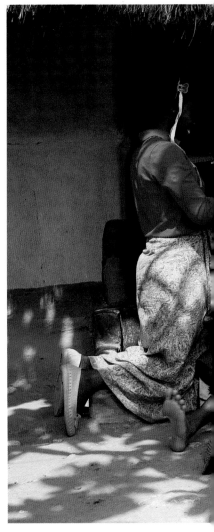

The traditional method for grinding maize is by pestle and mortar. Maize harvested is often placed in special storage bins within the village, (right) such as this one in Southern Province.

Hairdressing throughout Zimbabwe (left) is a sophisticated craft. All manner of intricate plaiting lends variety to the way in which a woman can wear her hair. Some of the more complicated styles can take twelve hours or more to complete, but once finished they will last for many weeks.

In rural Zimbabwe, man and his cattle are not easily separated. Cattle mean much more than meat and money to the owner. They buy his bride, pull his plough, fertilise his fields and give him security, as well as representing an important element in his spiritual life. But the special status enjoyed by cattle has its disadvantages. The density of the cattle population has caused over-grazing and erosion. In many areas, the land simply cannot tolerate the burden much longer.

PREVIOUS PAGE: *Rural Zimbabwe can be spectacularly beautiful to the visitor. Here, the granite cliffs of the Honde valley dwarf a tiny settlement in the north east of the country. The bulk of the manual work in the countryside is carried out by women, who often toil for sixteen hours without rest.*

For generations western clothes have been a familiar sight. This woman (left) lives in a village on the edge of Hwange National Park, and the stylish dress is a direct result of her husband's employment - he works as a guide for tourists who have come to view game.

In the remote countryside, cars can be murderously expensive and difficult to maintain, so policemen (above) often find that they can perform their duties just as effectively on bicycles.

Wildlife in the countryside is increasingly regarded by locals as something other than a source of food. This girl (above, opposite) lives just to the south of the Matuzviadonha Game Reserve, and her father made the elephant carving for her - a sign, some would suggest, of a growing awareness of the need to conserve such species.

Despite many hours of tedious and back-breaking work, these rural workers near Masvingo (below, opposite) can still show visitors welcoming smile.

PREVIOUS PAGE: *The boy who owns a football is often the most popular in the village. Here sweat and dust mingle freely on a makeshift pitch just outside the town of Mvuma in Midlands Province.*

Recent years have seen massive investment in education throughout the countryside. Zimbabwe enjoys the highest literacy rate in sub-Saharan Africa, and the general level of education is so good that young Zimbabweans are frequently over-qualified for the jobs that are immediately open to them.

St. Augustine's Mission, Penhalonga, is typical of many to be found in the country. Often linked to funding agencies in Europe and America, they tend to enjoy better facilities than the government schools. Teachers often come to such institutions from abroad for a few years before returning home; others will stay for life. Missionaries have been active from the middle of the last century, and their impact on the intellectual life of the country has been substantial. Many of Zimbabwe's leading political and industrial figures are mission-educated.

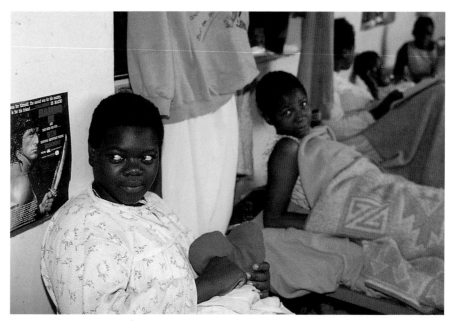

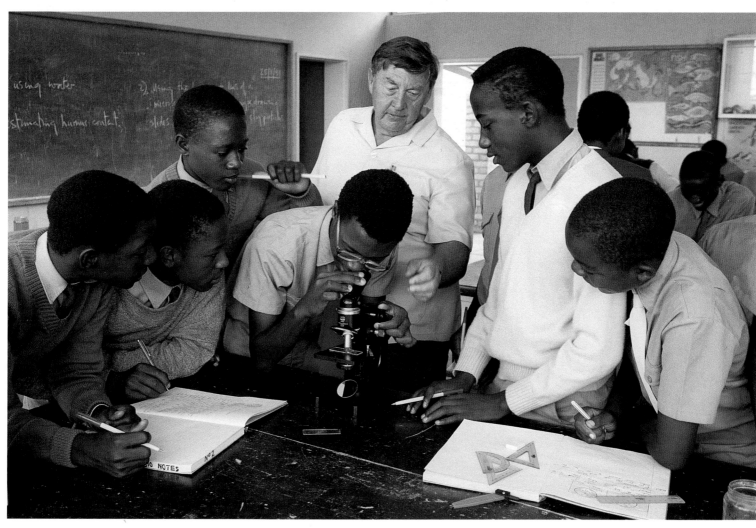

PROTECTING THE FUTURE

The outstanding feature of Zimbabwe's natural heritage is its variety, for few nations in Africa can boast such a wide range of terrain. The country is bounded in the north by the Zambezi river, which has been damned at Kariba to make an immense freshwater take. Further upstream are the Victoria Falls, the largest curtain of falling water anywhere in the world. Bordering Mozambique in the east is a range of mountains reaching 2,600 metres at their highest point, which are not only productive but very beautiful. To the south is the dry, flat landscape of the lowveld, broken by huge swathes of irrigated sugar cane, wheat and cotton. At the western edge of this plateau near Bulawayo are the Matopo Hills, a craggy jumble of granite outcrops punctuated by huge rocks which balance precariously on top of one another. Between this other-worldly landscape and the Victoria Falls is a sandy plain of monotonous flatness marking the eastern fringe of the Kalahari Desert. What it lacks in topography it makes up for in wildlife. This is the Hwange National Park, one of the most famous game reserves in Africa.

Despite the huge variety of landscapes within Zimbabwe's borders, it is a remarkably compact country. Unlike neighbouring Zambia, which sprawls awkwardly in two bulbous lumps across the south of the continent, Zimbabwe is almost circular in shape, making internal communication straightforward. Yet the very ease with which farmers, prospectors and foresters can move around the land has made it peculiarly vulnerable to depletion. One example is intensive grazing by cattle which can simply move on to the next patch of good grass. The extensive deforestation of the country is another.

The most immediate issue concerning Zimbabwe's natural resources is the sheer number of people which the land must support. Improvements in health care have meant that more children are surviving than ever before, and Zimbabwe's population growth is among the highest in the world. The onerous effects of this are felt everywhere, not just in social services but in the very use of the land itself, where most Zimbabweans still live.

The depletion of the land has been made worse by the distribution of Zimbabwe's people. Before Independence, land was divided along racial lines, with Africans allocated the poorest and hilliest terrain. The legacy of this policy is likely to last well into the next century, and it puts a very uneven burden on the country's natural resources. Over the years, those forced to live in the poorer regions have placed intolerable strains on their land, denuding it of trees and grass cover. In some areas soil has become insufficient to grow the staple maize crop. Small dams, fed by large catchments which are subject to severe erosion, can silt up in as little as five years.

In response, the government has taken decisive action at the heart of the matter. Not only is there a programme to redistribute the land under way, but the Health Ministry is reporting a strong response to their advocacy of family planning. At the same time, development programmes have been designed to make the communal areas more attractive and productive. Efforts have been made to create 'growth points' in many parts of the country. Here, private enterprise is encouraged to participate in the development of commercial and manufacturing activity by providing employment, goods and services for the local communities. The National Conservation Strategy, adopted by the government, acknowledges the importance of a comprehensive population policy, for the use of the country's natural resources hinges directly on the human burden which those resources have to bear.

PREVIOUS PAGE: *After 40 years under water, the teak forest is still standing, its skeletal branches jutting into the sky from another world.*

Lake Kariba is the third largest man-made reservoir in the world, running nearly 300 kilometres from one end to the other and 42 kilometres at its broadest. It was created when the Zambezi was dammed for the purpose of generating hydro-electric power, but the incidental beauty of the flooded valley makes it a major attraction.

The Lake is now important for the tourist income which it generates; locally built luxury cruisers as well as humbler maritime craft are available for hire.

Commercial fishing is also important, the catch appearing on restaurant tables as far away as Masvingo and Bulawayo at the other end of the country.

FOLLOWING PAGE: *Bumi Hills is an exclusive safari camp which clings to the side of the Matuzviadonha Game reserve. Several other camps are to be found along the lakeshore - and even in the form of houseboats on the lake itself.*

Four hundred kilometres downstream of the Victoria Falls is a very different Zambezi from the one that excites white water rafters. The wilderness areas of Mana Pools must be some of the most spectacular in Africa, and have been recognised as a World Heritage Site. Canoeing from Kariba Dam to the borders of Mozambique offers an appreciation of nature unsullied by the sound of the internal combustion engine.

The ancient flood plain through which the Zambezi labours, broad and sluggish, makes for open horizons and big landscapes. On the Acacia Albida which dominate both banks of the river, the browse line of the elephants is clearly visible. Quite often when the acacias bear fruit, elephants can be seen standing on their hind legs reaching with their trunks into the branches. The prize is the fruit of these trees, a gourmet food on the elephantine menu.

The Eastern Highlands are a range of mountains running some three hundred kilometres from north to south, quite striking in their variety and beauty. Forming a natural border with Mozambique, they extend from the gently rolling countryside near Nyanga to the jagged dog teeth of Chimanimani, and include the highest mountains in the country. The loftiest peak of all is Inyangani, which takes its name from n'anga, a local medicine man of legendary powers. At 2,592 metres above sea level, Inyangani's trees and grasses are trimmed with frost during the winter months, and the chill air is invigorating. Further down in the valley the mild climate is ideal for the commercial cultivation of coffee, tea, pine, wattle, gum, flowers and grapes.

The gorgeous scenery and cool air of the Highlands make them a natural holiday destination. Trout fishing, golf, bowls and horse riding are all possible, and there are several international-class hotels. Should walking ever cease to be a chore for most Africans, the Eastern Highlands may one day fulfil their potential as some of the best hiking land on the continent. Most of the peaks can be conquered with little mountaineering skill, and they are punctuated by hundreds of rivers, waterfalls and deceptively chilly pools to entice the foolhardy.

Gold deposits in the Eastern Highlands were some of the first to be commercially extracted in the country. In the middle of the century there was a marked slump in activity before improved technology began to pay dividends once more. Ancient timbers of a long-silent stamping mill recall pioneering days at Penhalonga, some twenty kilometres east of Mutare. Beneath the gleam of iron pyrites at this old dump, just a residue of gold remains to be extracted by modern methods. Nearby, Redwing Mine is now one of the most productive in the country.

The Eastern Highlands are blessed with many picturesque streams and waterfalls, but some have a reputation for being dangerous. The Nyangombe Falls (far left) may be inviting, but the rocks are very smooth, and several adventurous visitors have slipped to their death.

The Vumba Gardens are a well-kept secret lying just a few minutes' drive from the centre of Mutare. Formerly the Manchester Gardens, they were the creation of a colonial mayor and his wife who once lived in the foothills overlooking the town. To this day the gardens, which are now run by the National Parks, have been immaculately maintained an achievement all the more remarkable for the fact that the region was seriously affected by the Liberation War. Surrounding a neatly-trimmed lawn, shrubs and trees gathered from all over the world vie for attention while huge waterlillies float on an ornamental lake. From ten in the morning until four in the afternoon, tea is served in the gardens.

The Chimanimani Mountains at the southern end of the Eastern Highlands are formed by alternate layers of quartzites and schists, giving a much more jagged appearance than the rounded forms of the granite and dolerite mountains to the north. The Bridal Veil Falls (left) are a short distance from the town of Chimanimani.

Gonarezhou National Park is the second largest in Zimbabwe after Hwange, covering 496,000 hectares. The name translated informs us of the presence of elephants.

The largest elephants in Zimbabwe have been recorded here, but poaching in recent years has taken its toll. However, with tourism flourishing, the money has now become available to deter the organised gangs that, at one time, were left unharassed to continue with their illegal trade.

The Chilojo Cliffs (right) only give a suggestion of the magnificence of this rarely visited park. The riverine woodlands and the different habitats of the nyala antelopes are some of the most outstanding scenery to be found in the country. Camps, mainly thatched cottages, are slowly opening up in the park but the view from their windows is that of the last millennium.

The flowers (below) are known locally as the Save Star.

Matopos is an easy drive from Bulawayo, but the moment you arrive another Africa descends upon you. This ancient and primeval place is as holy as any cathedral, for here the ancestral spirits watch over the living world. Six years before he died, Cecil Rhodes had gone riding among the knobbly crags of these granite hills. So overwhelmed was he by their power and beauty that he asked to be buried here in his will. When in 1902 he died in Cape Town, his body was dispatched by train to Bulawayo before being hauled into the very heart of this magical landscape.

Few individuals have left such a deep imprint on the history of Africa as Cecil John Rhodes. "My strongest belief is in power," he once declared. "But what is the end of power? So often desert sand or ruins. But there is a force... a vitality that drives me on, and one cannot evade it if one would."

Not far from Rhodes' grave there are many fine paintings, daubed onto the rocks by an ancient people who would never have understood such preoccupations.

190